Volume equivalents

IMPERIAL	METRIC	IMPERIAL	METRIC
1fl oz	30ml	15fl oz	450ml
2fl oz	60ml	16fl oz	500ml
2½fl oz	75ml	2 cups	500ml
3½fl oz	100ml	1 pint	500ml
4fl oz	120ml	3 cups	700ml
5fl oz	150ml	4 cups	950ml
6fl oz	175ml	2 pints	950ml
7fl oz	200ml	2 pints	roughly 1 liter
8fl oz	250ml	2½ pints	1.2 liters
10fl oz	300ml	3 pints	1.4 liters
12fl oz	350ml	3.5 pints	1.7 liters
14fl oz	400ml	4 pints	1.8 liters

Weight equivalents

IMPERIAL	METRIC	IMPERIAL	METRIC
½oz	15g	5½oz	150g
¾oz	20g	6oz	175g
scant 1oz	25g	7oz	200g
1oz	30g	8oz	225g
1½oz	45g	9oz	250g
1⅓oz	50g	10oz	300g
2oz	60g	1lb	450g
2½oz	75g	1lb 2oz	500g
3oz	85g	1½lb	675g
3½oz	100g	2lb	900g
4oz	115g	2¼lb	1kg
4½oz	125g	3lb 3oz	1.5kg
5oz	140g	4lb	1.8kg

everyday easy
Chicken

Based on content previously published in
The Illustrated Kitchen Bible

everyday easy
Chicken

simple suppers • roasts • one-pot • leftovers

DK

LONDON, NEW YORK, MELBOURNE,
MUNICH, AND DELHI

US Editor
Beth Hester

Editor
Andrew Roff

Designer
Kathryn Wilding

Senior Jacket Creative
Nicola Powling

Managing Editor
Dawn Henderson

Managing Art Editor
Christine Keilty

Production Editor
Ben Marcus

Production Controller
Hema Gohil

Creative Technical Support
Sonia Charbonnier

DK INDIA

Head of Publishing
Aparna Sharma

Design Manager
Romi Chakraborty

Designer
Neha Ahuja

DTP Coordinator
Balwant Singh

DTP Designer
Tarun Sharma

Material first published in *The Illustrated Kitchen Bible* in 2008
This edition first published in the United States
by DK Publishing, 375 Hudson Street
New York, New York 10014

09 10 11 12   10 9 8 7 6 5 4 3 2 1

176448—October 2009

Copyright © 2008, 2009 Dorling Kindersley
Text copyright © 2008, 2009 Dorling Kindersley
All rights reserved

A catalog record for this book is available from the Library of Congress.

ISBN 978-0-7566-5792-5

DK books are available at special discounts when purchased in bulk for sales
promotions, premiums, fund-raising, or educational use. For details, contact:
DK Publishing Special Markets, 375 Hudson Street, New York,
New York 10014 or SpecialSales@dk.com.

Color reproduction by MDP, Bath, UK
Printed and bound in Singapore by Star Standard

Discover more at
www.dk.com

CONTENTS

We all love chicken. Many cultures around the world enjoy classic chicken dishes as part of their cuisine—whether Indian Chicken Tikka Masala, Southern Fried Chicken, or Thai Noodle Stir-fry. The really great news is that most of these are easy to make at home when you're shown how. Chicken is great for any occasion too—from a fast family supper to an impressive main dish when entertaining—so knowing your wishbone from your drumstick can drastically increase your culinary repertoire. Easy to cook, healthy, and readily available, the benefits of being a chicken whiz are manifold.

Other poultry is equally delicious, so we've included some here too. Turkey, goose, poussin, and duck are all readily available and are worth the extra expense. Game meats, such as pheasant and guinea fowl, although more occasional dishes, are thoroughly rewarding to cook and eat.

A range of chicken **Techniques** at the beginning of the book, including boning, butterflying, marinating, poaching, braising, roasting, and carving, will refine your core skills, enabling you to save time in the kitchen. Following this is a range of **Recipe Planners** that showcase recipes Ready in 30 Minutes, Healthy, Budget, Prepare Ahead, Spicy, or Light so cooks in a hurry can easily find something right for every occasion.

A selection of hors d'oeuvres and bite-sized finger food in the **Eat With Your Fingers** section gives great ideas for starting a meal when entertaining, creating an informal buffet, or taking on a picnic. Serve Chicken Liver Pâté to guarantee a flying start to an informal dinner party or add Chicken Croustades to a buffet-style luncheon—it's sure to be the most popular dish on the table.

Simple Suppers includes recipes that you can easily make in the evening on a hectic weekday, including Chicken Breasts in Garlic Sauce, Chicken Jalfrezi, and Devilled Turkey. These recipes require just a few ingredients and take minimal time to prepare. Simple and tasty, they are guaranteed to become family favorites that you can whip up in no time.

If you want to enjoy a delicious meal without having to wash lots of dishes afterward, choose something from the **One-pot** section. Coq au Vin and Chicken Pot Pie in particular are one-pot classics. Put all the ingredients together in a pot, leave to bubble in the oven or on the stove, and wait for the mouth-watering results.

Chicken has a formal side, too—it can be the perfect choice to cook for friends. It partners well with a number of flavors, in dishes such as Chicken with Pancetta, and textures, in dishes such as Creamy Tarragon Chicken, to give many luxurious meals, all explained in the **Supper for Friends** section.

For many people, a Sunday wouldn't be the same without a roast. And with the wealth of recipes in the **Roasts** section, why save it for just one day a week? Make any of these classic roast recipes, including Roast Chicken and Chicken in a Pot, or try something a little different—treat the family to French Roast Chicken or Roast Chicken with Thyme and Lemon.

If you plan your meals you can easily make a whole chicken last several days. Make one of the recipes in the **Leftovers** section, such as Calzone or Chicken Pasties, as a delicious way to use up any remaining poultry or other leftover ingredients in the fridge. A meal made from leftovers can often be as great as the meal that produced them!

Add some vegetables or other side dishes to your meal with the recipes in the **Accompaniments** section, including Ultimate Mashed Potatoes and Egg Fried Rice, and you have everything you need to make a spectacular chicken dinner.

Give all of these recipes a try and see just how easy it is to enjoy chicken and other poultry every day.

A guide to symbols

The recipes in this book are accompanied by symbols that alert you to important information.

 Tells you how many people the recipe serves, or the quantity.

 Indicates how much time you will need to prepare and cook a dish. Next to this symbol you will also find out if additional time is required for such things as marinating, standing, or cooling. You will have to read the recipe to find out exactly how much extra time is needed.

 Points out nutritional benefits, such as low fat or low GI (Glycemic Index).

 This important alert refers to preparation work that must be done before you can begin to cook the recipe. For example, you may need to soak some beans overnight.

 This denotes special equipment that is required, such as a deep-fat fryer or skewers. Where possible, alternatives are given.

 This symbol accompanies freezing information.

Roasting Poultry

Use these times as a guide, bearing in mind that the size and weight of each bird vary. Be sure to preheat the oven before cooking your bird(s), and always check that the bird is fully cooked before serving.

MEAT		OVEN TEMPERATURE	COOKING TIME
Poussin		375°F (190°C)	12 mins per 1lb (450g) plus 12 mins
Chicken		400°F (200°C)	20 mins per 1lb (450g) plus 20 mins
Duck		350°F (180°C)	20 mins per 1lb (450g) plus 20 mins
Goose		350°F (180°C)	20 mins per 1lb (450g) plus 20 mins
Pheasant		400°F (200°C)	50 mins total cooking
Turkey	7–9lb (3.5–4.5kg)	375°F (190°C)	2½–3 hrs total cooking
	10–12lb (5–6kg)	375°F (190°C)	3½–4 hrs total cooking
	13–17lb (6.5–8.5kg)	375°F (190°C)	4½–5 hrs total cooking

Choosing your chicken

Of all poultry, chicken is the most intensely reared. Age, exercise, and a good diet all add flavor—and, it must be said, expense—to chickens. Supermarkets and butchers sell many varieties of chicken that reflect all these conditions.

Common labels

Free-range birds should have access to daytime open-air runs for at least half their lives.

Traditional Free-range birds must be one of the slow-growing breeds. They cannot be stocked more than 4,000 in a house and more than 12 per 10 square feet.

Free-range Total Freedom birds, in addition to the traditional free-range specifications (above), should have unlimited open-air runs.

Organic birds must come from a farm recognized by an organic certification organization. They are fed organic grains and soybeans, cannot be treated with drugs or antibiotics, and must have outdoor access.

Common classifications

Stewing chicken refers to female chickens over 10 months old and weighing over 3lb (1.35kg). They are great for stewing and poaching.

Chicken—depending on whether the bird is free-range or not, chickens are slaughtered between $5^{1}/_{4}$ to $11^{1}/_{2}$ weeks of age. They weigh around 3lb 3oz (1.5kg).

Poussin are young chickens less than 28 days old, weighing 12oz–1lb (340–450g). These are tender birds that are great roasted or butterflied on a barbecue.

Put your wrapped bird on a rimmed plate in the bottom of the refrigerator. Don't let any raw juices drip and observe the use-by date.

Stewing chicken

Chicken

Poussin

TECHNIQUES

Cut up a chicken

Poultry is often left whole for roasting, poaching, and slow-cooking in a pot. For other cooking methods, cut birds into 4 or 8 pieces. For 4 pieces, work to step 6, and for 8 pieces, continue to step 8.

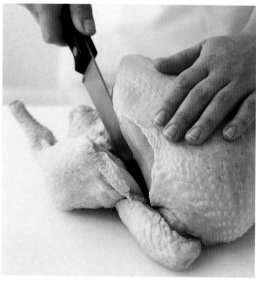

1 Remove the wishbone, then place the bird breast-side up on a cutting board. Using a chef's knife, cut down and through the thigh joint to separate the leg from the rest of the body.

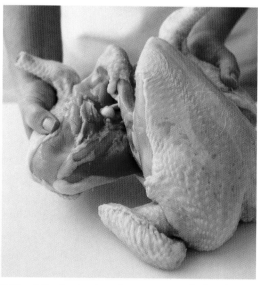

2 Bend the leg back as far as you can to break the leg joint. When the ball is free from the socket, you will hear a pop. Cut the leg away from the backbone, then repeat with the other leg.

3 Fully extend one wing, then use sharp poultry shears to cut off the wing tip at the second joint. Repeat to remove the other wing tip.

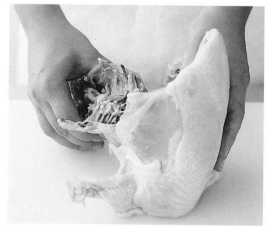

4 Using your hands, firmly grasp the backbone, and break it away from the breast section.

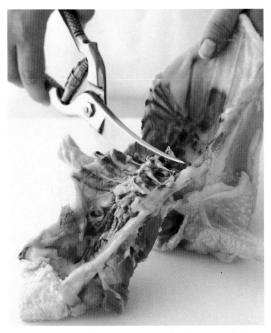

5 Using poultry shears, remove the lower end of the backbone (which has no flesh attached to it) from the remaining breast section.

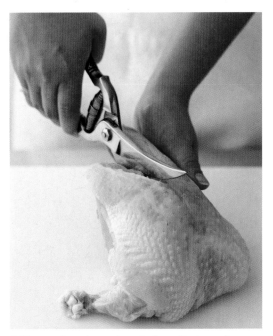

6 Use poultry shears to cut along the breastbone from top to bottom. Trim unwanted sections of breastbone. The chicken is now cut into 4 pieces.

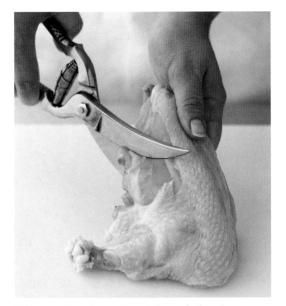

7 Use poultry shears to cut through the ribs two-thirds of the way along each breast diagonally, producing two breast pieces, one with a wing. Repeat with the other whole breast.

8 Cut each leg through the joint above the drumstick that connects it to the thigh, and cut through to separate. Repeat with the other leg. The chicken is now cut into 8 pieces.

Boning

For quickly cooked dishes or recipes that call for poultry to be flattened, the bones must first be removed.

Detach the breast

1 Using poultry shears, cut away the ribs and backbone. Work from the thickest wing end of the breast toward the narrowest end.

2 Using a boning knife, separate the flesh from the bone by following the contours of the breastbone to cut the fillet off. Use the breastbone to flavor stock, if you wish (see page 168).

Bone a leg

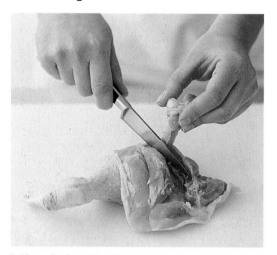

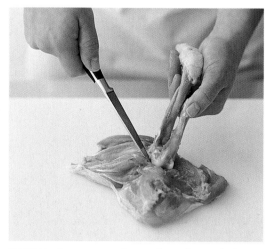

1 Place the leg skin-side down on a cutting board. Using a sharp knife, cut halfway through the flesh at the top of the thigh bone. Cut along to the knuckle and ease the bone away. Repeat on the drumstick.

2 Lift the bones up and away from the central knuckle joint. Using short strokes with the tip of your knife, remove the 2 bones from the flesh. Use to flavor stock or discard (see page 168).

Bone a thigh

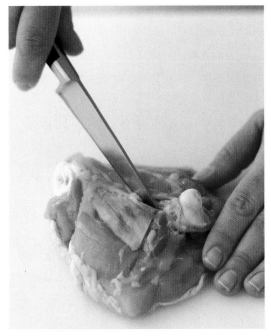

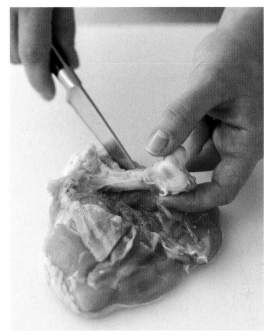

1 Place the thigh skin-side down on a cutting board. Use a small, sharp boning or paring knife to locate the bone at one end.

2 Cut an incision through the flesh, following the contour of the exposed bone. Cut around the bone to cut it completely free from the flesh, and discard or use to flavor stock (see page 168).

Bone a drumstick

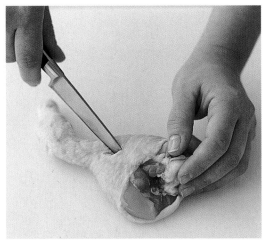

1 Starting in the middle of the drumstick, insert the tip of your knife until you locate the bone. Slice along the bone in both directions to expose it fully.

2 Open the flesh and neatly cut around the bone to free it completely from the flesh, and discard, or use to flavor stock (see page 168).

Butterfly

Ideal for grilling or broiling, this preparation for small poultry, such as Cornish hens, flattens the bird to ensure even cooking.

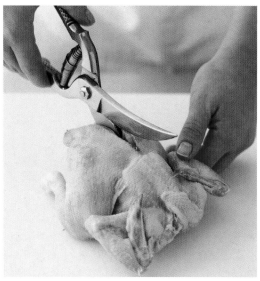

1 Place the bird breast-side down on a sturdy cutting board. Using poultry shears, cut along both sides of the backbone, remove it completely, and discard or use for stock. Open the bird and turn it over.

2 Using the heel of one hand and the other hand to stabilize, press down firmly to crush the breastbone. Once flattened, use a sharp knife to cut slits into the legs and thighs to ensure even cooking.

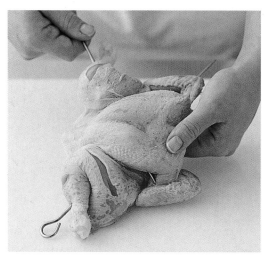

3 Carefully push a metal skewer diagonally through the left leg to the right wing, then a second skewer through the right leg to the left wing.

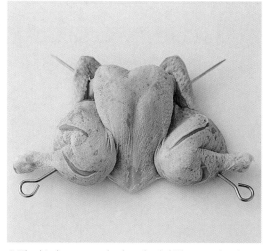

4 The bird can now be brushed with a marinade, then grilled, broiled, or roasted in the oven. Remove the skewers and carve the bird before serving.

Marinate

Using a marinade will produce tender and flavorful chicken.

Mix the ingredients of your marinade in a bowl. In a separate bowl, large enough to hold the chicken in a single layer, coat the chicken with the marinade, turning the pieces to coat it all over. Cover the bowl with plastic wrap, and chill in the refrigerator for an hour or more, depending on the marinade and the time available.

Stuff a boneless chicken breast

Don't overstuff the chicken breasts—it will increase the risk of leakage.

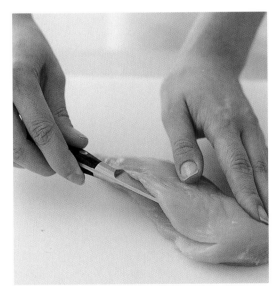

1 Using a sharp knife, cut a pocket about 1½in (4cm) deep into the side of the breast fillet. Make your cut so that both sides of the pocket are the same thickness, which will ensure even cooking.

2 Gently press the stuffing into the pocket, and roll back the flesh to enclose it. Secure with a toothpick. Rolling the stuffed fillet in a crumb coating before cooking will help seal the pocket.

Steeping

The meat produced by steeping is popular in Chinese cooking. First, simmer your chicken in stock or water, then remove from the heat. As the water cools, the meat gently cooks and becomes extremely tender.

1 Choose either stock or water to steep your chicken. Place the bird in a large pot and cover with the liquid.

2 Add some green onions and bring to a boil, then cover with a tight-fitting lid and simmer for 20 minutes. Remove the pot from the heat and leave for around 1 hour with the lid still tightly fitted.

3 Remove the chicken from the pot and pierce the thickest part of the leg. If the juices run clear, the chicken is done. Place into a large bowl of iced cold water. Leave until completely cool.

4 Remove the chicken from the water and drain well. Place the bird on a cutting board and carve according to your recipe.

Poaching

Don't allow the liquid to boil—keep it simmering for delicate meat. Try adding some vegetables to the pot to make a roast with a difference.

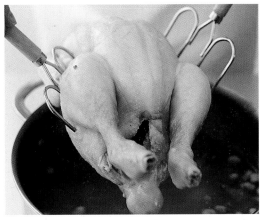

1 Place your chicken in a pan and add water until just covered. Remove the chicken and bring the water to the boil. Add a pinch of salt and replace the chicken, cover, and leave to simmer for 35 minutes.

2 The bird is cooked when the juices run clear when the leg is skewered in its thickest part. If the juices are red, return to the pan for another 10 minutes. Remove the bird from the pan and carve.

Braising and pot-roasting

The rich flavors produced by braising and pot-roasting chicken make them ideal techniques if you want to make a flavor-packed dish with minimal effort.

1 Cut a chicken into 8 pieces and season with salt and pepper (see page 12). Heat about 1oz (30g) butter in a heavy saucepan and add the chicken. Turn the chicken and cook until golden.

2 Stir in 1 tbsp plain flour and cook for 2 minutes. Stir in 1 tbsp passata, 8fl oz (250ml) red wine, and 1 tbsp sugar, and bring to a boil. Turn the heat down, cover, and cook for 50 minutes or until done.

Roasting

This favorite technique takes minutes to prepare and, if you follow a few golden rules, promises fantastic results. For cooking times, see page 8.

1 Put the raw bird on a large, clean cutting board and pull the skin back from around the neck cavity. Locate the wishbone with your finger and work it loose by gently moving your finger back and forth.

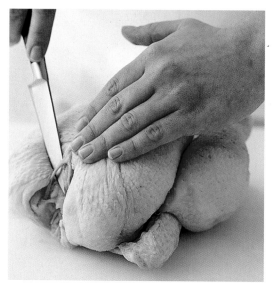

2 Insert a small, sharp knife behind the bone and gently work it down to the bottom of one of the wishbone's "arms," then cut it free from the flesh. In an older chicken, the wishbone will be quite strong.

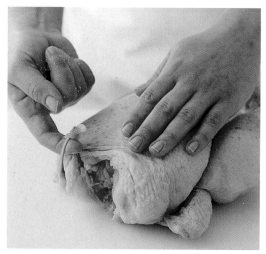

3 Pull the wishbone out by hooking your finger under the center and gently tugging until it comes free. Removing the wishbone before roasting makes the bird much easier to carve when serving.

4 Smear butter or rub oil all over the outside of the bird, then season well with salt and pepper inside and out. (If you are stuffing the bird, push the stuffing under the breast skin.)

5 Baste the chicken at regular intervals while it roasts. Turn the bird breast-side down after the first 30 minutes of the cooking time so the juices help baste the breast meat.

6 Turn the chicken breast-side up for the last 20 minutes of the cooking time to crisp and brown the skin. The bird is cooked when the juices run clear when the leg is skewered in its thickest part.

Add stuffing

1 Before cooking the bird, blend together stuffing ingredients in a bowl. (Butter, one egg, fresh bread crumbs, chopped parsley, and lemon zest are shown here.) Season with salt and pepper.

2 Carefully ease the skin away from the breast and gently push the stuffing under the skin from the neck end. This ensures the stuffing cooks through.

Resting and carving

Leaving a roast to rest is very important. It allows the juices to flow to all parts of the bird so every slice will be as flavorful as the last.

1 Transfer the bird to a cutting board, breast-side up, cover with foil, and let rest in a warm place for 15 minutes. This allows the juices to flow throughout the bird and keep the meat moist.

2 To carve the bird, remove the legs by cutting the skin between the leg and the body and pushing the blade down to where the leg bone joins the body. It is easiest if you angle the blade into the body slightly.

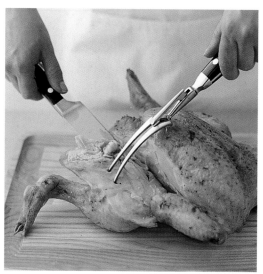

3 Work the blade from side to side to loosen the joint, then, with a slight sawing motion, push the blade through the joint, cutting the leg free. Transfer the leg to a warmed plate and repeat with the other leg.

4 Remove a breast by cutting as if you are dividing the bird in half, just to one side of the breastbone. As the blade hits the bone, cut along it to remove all the meat; repeat on the other side.

5 Place one breast cut-side down on the cutting board. Slice the breast horizontally, leaving the wing with a piece of breast meat attached.

6 Carve each leg by cutting it in half through the joint at the midway point. As you reach the joint, work the blade into the joint to separate the pieces.

Make gravy

1 Using a large spoon, skim off most of the fat from the pan juices. Mix 1 tbsp all-purpose flour with 1 tbsp of the chicken fat.

2 Put the roasting pan over low heat. Whisk in the fat mixture. Add 1¼ cups stock or water and bring to a boil, whisking constantly. Strain and serve hot.

Ready in 30 minutes Make these recipes in half an hour or less.

Chicken croustades page 44

Devilled turkey page 82

Chicken and noodle stir-fry
page 182

**Smoked chicken mousse on
endive** page 50

Garlicky turkey burgers page 88

Warm chicken salad page 180

Turkey à la king page 80

Chicken chow mein page 186

Thai green chicken curry
page 70

Healthy These recipes are all low in fat or low GI.

Thai noodle stir-fry page 62

Mexican chicken noodle soup
page 178

Chicken cacciatore page 106

Roast chicken page 154

Chicken biryani page 132

Baked poussin with lemon and paprika page 118

Cock-a-leekie soup page 176

Chicken jalfrezi page 84

Chinese rice porridge page 192

Roast turkey with spiked gravy page 164

Chicken with thyme and lemon
page 158

27

Budget All use less expensive cuts of a bird or other inexpensive ingredients.

Southern fried chicken page 66

Chicken croustades page 44

Coronation chicken rolls
page 52

Honey mustard barbecued chicken page 54

Chicken chow mein page 186

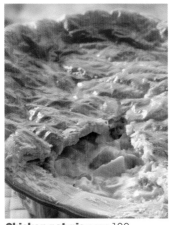

Chicken pot pie page 100

Cock-a-leekie soup page 176

Chicken croquettes page 184

Chicken jalousie page 190

Garlicky turkey burgers page 88

Chicken korma page 104

Chicken tikka masala page 108

Tandoori chicken page 134

Calzone page 174

Chicken liver pâté page 40

Prepare ahead Make these dishes in advance, before you plan to serve.

Rustic meat terrine page 38

Chicken croquettes page 184

Turkey à la king page 80

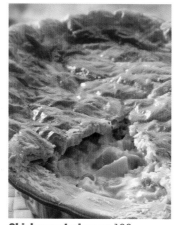

Chicken pot pie page 100

Chicken tikka masala page 108

Coq au vin page 112

Chinese rice porridge page 192

Chicken liver pâté page 40

Duck confit page 116

Thai green chicken curry
page 70

Chicken jalfrezi page 84

Chicken and apricot tagine
page 102

Spicy If you have a taste for something with a kick, choose one of these.

Thai noodle stir-fry page 62

Devilled turkey page 82

Chicken tikka masala page 108

Couscous royale page 92

Chicken korma page 104

Chicken piri-piri page 94

Thai green chicken curry
page 70

Spicy orange duck page 142

Garlicky turkey burgers page 88   **Chicken biryani** page 132

Jambalaya page 98

Guinea hen with spiced lentils
page 138

Chicken jalfrezi page 84

33

Light For lunches, snacks, and light suppers, choose one of these tasty bites.

Warm chicken salad page 180

Chicken satay page 48

Cock-a-leekie soup page 176

Chicken with herb sauce
page 78

Turkey cutlets with artichokes
page 86

Chicken in balsamic vinegar page 124

Turkey kebabs page 58

Lemon honey chicken breasts with mustard mayonnaise page 140

Smoked chicken mousse on endive page 50

Chicken and noodle stir-fry page 182

Chicken croustades page 44

Chicken wrapped in pancetta and sage page 136

Saffron chicken brochettes page 56

EAT WITH YOUR FINGERS

Rustic meat terrine

Full of flavor and texture, this pâté is extremely versatile.

INGREDIENTS

12oz (350g) sliced bacon
9oz (250g) chicken livers, trimmed
1lb (450g) ground veal
12oz (300g) ground pork
8 tbsp butter, melted and cooled
½ cup dry sherry
1 onion, finely chopped
2 garlic cloves, minced
1 tsp dried oregano
½ tsp ground allspice
salt and freshly ground black pepper

METHOD

1 Preheat the oven to 350°F (180°C). Line a 6 cup terrine mold or loaf pan with the bacon slices, letting the ends of the bacon hang over the sides of the dish.

2 Pulse the chicken livers in a food processor until finely chopped. Transfer to a bowl. Add the veal, pork, butter, sherry, onion, garlic, oregano, and allspice and season well with salt and pepper. Mix with your hands until combined.

3 Transfer the meat mixture to the terrine mold and fold the bacon ends over the top. Cover tightly with the lid or aluminum foil. Place the dish in a roasting pan and add enough hot water to come halfway up the sides of the dish.

4 Bake for 1½ hours, until a meat thermometer inserted in the center reads 165°F (74°C). Transfer the terrine in its mold to a baking sheet. Replace the foil with a fresh sheet. Place another pan to fit inside the terrine, and fill with heavy cans of food. Refrigerate for 24 hours. Unmold, slice, and serve.

GOOD WITH Slices of warm crusty bread or toast, and plenty of Dijon mustard and small sour pickles (cornichons).

PREPARE AHEAD After pressing, the unmolded terrine can be wrapped and refrigerated for up to 5 days.

8 servings

**prep 30 mins
• cook 1½ hrs,
plus pressing**

**6 cup terrine
mold or loaf pan**

**freeze for up to
1 month**

Chicken liver pâté

Red wine adds flavor to this spread and cuts through the richness of the liver.

INGREDIENTS

12oz (350g) chicken livers
8 tbsp butter
²/₃ cup hearty red wine
2 tbsp chopped chives
¼ tsp dried thyme
salt and freshly ground pepper
sprigs of fresh thyme, to garnish

METHOD

1 Rinse the livers and pat dry with paper towels. Trim away any sinew or greenish portions from the livers with kitchen scissors, then cut each in half.

2 Melt 4 tbsp butter in a large frying pan over medium heat. Add the livers and cook, stirring occasionally, for about 4 minutes, or until browned.

3 Add the wine, chives, and thyme to the pan. Bring to a boil. Cook, stirring occasionally, for 4 minutes, or until the liquid is reduced by about half and the livers are just cooked through when sliced open.

4 Remove the pan from the heat and let cool for 10 minutes. Transfer the contents of the pan to a food processor. Process until smooth. Season with salt and pepper. Spoon the pâté into a serving bowl, pressing it down with the back of the spoon after each addition so that it is firmly packed.

5 Melt the remaining butter over medium heat. Pour it over the top of the pâté. Refrigerate, uncovered, for at least 2 hours. Garnish with sprigs of fresh thyme and serve.

GOOD WITH Plenty of toasted French breach slices and cornichon pickles.

PREPARE AHEAD The pâté is best refrigerated for 2 days before serving to develop the flavors.

4 servings

prep 10 mins, plus cooling and chilling • cook 15 mins

the pâté can be frozen for up to 6 months

Smoked chicken and spinach filo triangles

These flaky parcels are delicious served hot or cold as an appetizer.

INGREDIENTS

1 tsp olive oil
8oz (225g) fresh spinach, washed, tough stems removed
4 scallions, white and green parts, finely chopped
4oz (115g) smoked chicken
$1^{1}/_{3}$ cup crème fraîche or heavy cream
1 tbsp chopped tarragon
1 tsp Dijon mustard
grated zest of 1 large lemon
$^{1}/_{2}$ cup toasted pine nuts
freshly ground black pepper
4 thawed frozen filo sheets
4 tbsp butter, melted
$^{1}/_{4}$ cup Parmesan cheese, grated

METHOD

1 Preheat the oven to 350°F (180°C). Heat the oil in a medium saucepan over medium heat. Add the spinach, cover, and cook about 5 minutes, until tender. Drain well and let cool. Pulse the spinach, scallions, smoked chicken, crème fraîche, tarragon, mustard, and lemon zest in a food processor until coarsely chopped. Stir in the pine nuts and season with pepper.

2 Line a baking sheet with wax paper. Place 1 filo sheet on the work surface, with the short side running horizontally. Cover the remaining filo with a damp paper towel to prevent drying. Brush the filo sheet with melted butter. Top with a second sheet and brush again with butter. Cut the filo pastry into three 4in (10cm) strips. Place a heaping spoonful of the chicken mixture about $^{1}/_{2}$in (13mm) below the top of a strip. Fold the right corner of the strip diagonally to the left to form a triangle that covers the filling. Fold the triangle with the filling down, and repeat folding down and over until you reach the end of the strip. Brush with butter and place on the baking sheet. Repeat with the other 3 strips, then with 2 more filo sheets and the remaining filling. Sprinkle with the Parmesan.

3 Transfer to a lightly oiled baking sheet. Bake for 20 minutes, until golden brown. Serve hot or warm.

GOOD WITH Your choice of dipping sauce.

PREPARE AHEAD The triangles can be covered and refrigerated for up to 1 day.

6 servings

prep 25 mins
• cook 20 mins

can be frozen
before baked

Chicken croustades

Tarragon and chicken is a popular combination.

INGREDIENTS

1 cooked chicken breast, skin removed
2 tbsp mayonnaise
1 tsp chopped tarragon, plus sprigs, to garnish
1 tsp whole-grain mustard
1 tsp fresh lemon juice
salt and freshly ground black pepper
12 croustade baskets

METHOD

1 Shred the chicken into small pieces.

2 Mix the mayonnaise, tarragon, mustard, and lemon juice together in a bowl. Add the chicken and mix again. Season with salt and pepper.

3 Divide the mixture among the croustades. Garnish each one with a tarragon sprig. Serve immediately.

PREPARE AHEAD The chicken filling can be refrigerated for several hours before using.

12 croustades

prep 15 mins

Baked BBQ wings with blue cheese dip

A variation on Buffalo wings, these sticky chicken wings are served with a tangy dip.

INGREDIENTS

2lb (900g) chicken wings
salt and freshly ground black pepper
2 tbsp olive oil
2 tbsp tomato paste
1 tbsp dried oregano
2 tsp light brown sugar
1 shallot, finely chopped
1 garlic clove, crushed
$\frac{1}{2}$ tsp hot red pepper sauce

For the blue cheese dip

$\frac{2}{3}$ cup sour cream
$\frac{1}{2}$ cup crumbled blue cheese, such
   as Roquefort or Danish blue
2 tbsp snipped chives
1 tbsp fresh lemon juice

METHOD

1 Season the wings with salt and pepper. Process the oil, tomato paste, oregano, brown sugar, shallot, garlic, and hot pepper sauce in a food processor until smooth. Combine the wings and sauce in a large self-sealing plastic bag, and coat the wings with the sauce. Let stand at room temperature for no more than 90 minutes.

2 Preheat the oven to 375°F (190°C). Spread the chicken on an oiled baking sheet. Bake for 20 minutes. Turn the wings and bake for 15 minutes more, until the wings show no sign of pink when pierced at the bone.

3 Meanwhile, mix the dip ingredients in a bowl. Serve the chicken wings hot, with the dip on the side, and a bowl to collect the bones.

PREPARE AHEAD The chicken can be coated in the tomato mixture and refrigerated for up to 6 hours.

4 servings

prep 20 mins,
plus marinating
• cook 25 mins

large self-
sealing plastic
food bag

Chicken satay

The authentic version is made with Indonesian soy sauce, *kecap manis*, but Chinese or Japanese soy sauce can also be used.

INGREDIENTS

3 boneless and skinless chicken breasts
2 tbsp kecap manis (available at Asian grocers) or soy sauce
4 tsp light or dark brown sugar
1 tbsp fresh lime juice
$^3/_4$in (2cm) piece fresh ginger, peeled and shredded
2 garlic cloves, crushed
2 tsp ground coriander
1 tsp minced lemongrass
$^1/_2$ tsp ground cumin
vegetable oil

For the satay sauce
1 cup (250g) smooth or chunky peanut butter
2 garlic cloves, finely chopped
$^3/_4$ cup well shaken coconut milk
1 tbsp soy sauce, preferably dark
1 tbsp dark brown sugar
$^1/_2$in (1cm) piece fresh ginger, peeled and shredded
1 tbsp fresh lemon juice
$^1/_8$ tsp cayenne pepper
salt and freshly ground pepper
lime wedges, for serving

METHOD

1 Cut the chicken into thin strips across the grain of the meat. Spread the strips out in a shallow, nonmetallic dish.

2 In a small bowl, mix kecap manis, brown sugar, lime juice, ginger, garlic, coriander, lemongrass, cumin, salt, and 2 tsp vegetable oil. Pour over the chicken and toss to coat. Cover the dish with plastic wrap and marinate in the refrigerator for at least 4 hours.

3 To make the satay sauce, put the peanut butter with half of the garlic in a small saucepan and cook over low heat for 2 minutes. Add the coconut milk, soy sauce, brown sugar, and ginger, and cook, stirring, for 2 minutes, or until heated through.

4 Add the lemon juice and remaining garlic, and season to taste with cayenne pepper, salt, and pepper. Let the sauce cool, cover with plastic wrap, and refrigerate.

5 When ready to cook, thread the chicken on the skewers. In a pan over low heat, reheat the satay sauce, stirring frequently.

6 Brush the chicken with oil and broil or grill on an outdoor grill for 5 minutes, turning over once or twice, until the chicken is opaque throughout. Garnish with lime wedges and serve hot with satay sauce.

PREPARE AHEAD The marinating chicken and the sauce can be refrigerated for up to 1 day.

6 servings

prep 20 mins, plus marinating • cook 5 mins

soak wooden skewers for 1 hour before use

wooden or metal skewers

EAT WITH YOUR FINGERS

Smoked chicken mousse on endive

Simple to make, these elegant hors d'oeuvres look wonderful and taste great.

INGREDIENTS

8oz (225g) smoked chicken breasts
3 tbsp mayonnaise
2 tbsp Dijon mustard
1 tbsp chopped tarragon
zest and juice of $\frac{1}{2}$ lemon
sea salt and freshly ground black pepper
2 Belgian endive
1 red Belgian endive
chopped chives, to garnish

METHOD

1 Discard the skin and bone from the smoked chicken. Dice the smoked chicken meat. Combine the chicken, mayonnaise, mustard, lemon zest and juice, and tarragon in a food processor and process until very finely chopped. Season with salt and pepper.

2 To serve, separate the endive leaves. Place spoonfuls of the mousse onto the ends of the wide ends of the endive leaves, and sprinkle with the chives. Serve immediately.

PREPARE AHEAD The mousse can be refrigerated for up to 1 day. The filled endive leaves should be served within 1 hour.

12 servings

prep 10 mins

Coronation chicken rolls

These rolls are synonymous with British summer picnics and garden parties.

INGREDIENTS

1 tbsp vegetable oil
1 shallot, finely chopped
1 tsp curry powder (either mild or hot,
   according to taste)
1 tbsp tomato paste
dash of Worcestershire sauce
½ cup (115g) mayonnaise
6 canned apricot halves in juice
2 cups diced cooked chicken
8 small rolls, preferably oval,
   split and spread with softened
   butter or left plain
2 tbsp chopped parsley

METHOD

1 Heat the oil in a small frying pan over medium-low heat. Add the shallot and cook for about 2 minutes until softened but not browned. Add the curry powder and stir for 1 minute until fragrant. Stir in the tomato paste and Worcestershire sauce. Remove from heat and let cool.

2 Process the shallot mixture, mayonnaise, and drained apricot halves in a food processor until smooth and creamy. Transfer to a bowl and stir in the chicken. Cover and refrigerate until needed.

3 Spoon the chicken salad onto the rolls, and sprinkle with the chopped parsley.

PREPARE AHEAD The chicken salad can be refrigerated up to 1 day in advance, then spooned on to the rolls an hour or two before serving.

12 sandwiches

**prep 15 mins,
plus cooling
• cook 5 mins**

Honey mustard barbecued chicken

The sweetness of honey and the tang of whole grain mustard combine to make a delicious glaze for barbecued chicken.

INGREDIENTS
8 chicken drumsticks or thighs
$\frac{1}{2}$ cup ketchup
$\frac{1}{2}$ cup orange juice
$\frac{1}{4}$ cup balsamic vinegar
2 tbsp olive oil
1 garlic clove, minced
1 tsp dried oregano
$\frac{1}{4}$ tsp ground black pepper

For the glaze
2 tbsp honey
2 tbsp whole grain mustard
grated zest of 1 lemon

METHOD
1 Make 2 or 3 deep cuts into each drumstick. Whisk the ketchup, orange juice, vinegar, olive oil, garlic, oregano, and pepper together in a nonmetallic bowl. Add the chicken and mix to coat well. Cover and refrigerate, occasionally turning the chicken, for at least 6 and up to 24 hours.

2 Build a medium fire in an outside grill. Remove the chicken from the marinade, reserving the marinade for basting. Lightly oil the grill grate. Place the chicken on the grill and cover. Grill for 20 minutes, turning and basting frequently with the marinade. Discard marinade.

3 To make the glaze, mix the honey, mustard, and lemon zest together. Brush the chicken with glaze and cook for 10–15 minutes more, or until the chicken juices are clear when pierced with the tip of a sharp knife.

GOOD WITH A crisp green salad and grilled corn on the cob.

PREPARE AHEAD Marinate the chicken for up to 24 hours.

4 servings

**prep 10 mins,
plus marinating
• cook 30 mins**

Saffron chicken brochettes

This simple preparation is ideal for a summer barbecue or as a bite-sized lunch.

INGREDIENTS
6 skinless, boneless chicken breasts 6oz (175g) each, cubed
2 red onions, thinly sliced
3 tbsp olive oil
zest and juice of 3 lemons
$\frac{1}{4}$ tsp crumbled saffron threads, dissolved in 1 tbsp of boiling water
salt and freshly ground black pepper
2 tbsp butter, melted
chopped basil, to garnish

METHOD
1 Put the chicken and onions in a large nonmetallic bowl. Whisk together the oil, lemon zest, the juice from 2 lemons and the saffron water. Season with salt and pepper. Pour over the chicken and onions, mix gently, and cover with plastic wrap. Refrigerate for at least 2 hours.

2 Mix the butter and the remaining lemon juice together.

3 Place an oiled rack 6in (15cm) from the heat. Preheat the broiler, and thread the chicken onto the skewers. Broil, turning occasionally, brushing with the butter mixture, about 10 minutes. Garnish with the basil and serve hot.

6 servings

prep 10 mins, plus marinating • cook 10 mins

soak wooden skewers for 1 hour before use

wooden or metal skewers

Turkey kebabs

Great tasting when cooked on a barbecue, you'll want to make these kebabs every week of the summer.

INGREDIENTS
$1/4$ cup soy sauce
2 tbsp olive oil
2 garlic cloves, finely chopped
$3/4$ tsp ground ginger
$1/4$ tsp crushed hot red pepper
$1^{1}/_{2}$lb (675g) skinless boneless turkey breasts,
   cut into 1in (2.5cm) cubes
1 red bell pepper, seeded and cut into
   1in (2.5cm) pieces
1 green bell pepper, seeded and cut into
   1in (2.5cm) pieces
1 large zucchini, cut into 1in (2.5cm) pieces

For the dip
250ml (8fl oz) plain yogurt
2 tbsp mint, chopped
$1/2$ tsp ground cumin

METHOD
1 Combine the soy sauce, oil, garlic, ginger, and red pepper flakes in a zippered plastic bag. Add the turkey and refrigerate for at least 1 hour.

2 Preheat the broiler. Thread the turkey, peppers, and zucchini onto skewers. Broil for 5–6 minutes on each side, or until cooked through.

3 Mix the yogurt, mint, and cumin; serve with the kebabs.

6 servings

**prep 20 mins,
plus marinating
• cook 10–12 mins**

**soak wooden
skewers for 1
hour before use**

**wooden or
metal skewers**

Thai noodle stir-fry

This fragrant and colorful stir-fry features the flavors of Thailand.

INGREDIENTS

6oz (75g) cellophane (mung bean) noodles

3 tbsp peanut or vegetable oil

3 skinless and boneless chicken breasts,
  cut into thin strips

1 onion, sliced

4oz (115g) shiitake mushrooms, sliced

1 red bell pepper, seeded and sliced

1 lemongrass stalk, peeled and bottom part minced

1 tsp peeled and finely grated fresh ginger

1 fresh hot Thai red chili, seeded and minced

1 head of bok choy, shredded

2 tbsp soy sauce

1 tbsp Asian fish sauce

1 tsp sweet chili sauce

METHOD

1 Soak the noodles in a bowl of very hot water about 10 minutes, until softened. Drain well and rinse under cold running water. Cut into manageable lengths with kitchen scissors.

2 Heat 2 tbsp of the oil in a wok over high heat. Add the chicken and stir-fry about 3 minutes, or until lightly browned. Transfer to a plate.

3 Reduce the heat to medium and add the remaining 1 tbsp oil. Add the onion and stir-fry for 2 minutes. Add the mushrooms, bell pepper, lemongrass, ginger, and chili, and stir-fry about 2 minutes, or until the bell pepper softens.

4 Add the bok choy and stir-fry for about 2 minutes, or until wilted. Return the chicken to the pan and add the noodles. Pour in the soy sauce, fish sauce, and sweet chili sauce, and toss everything together over the heat for 2–3 minutes, or until piping hot. Serve hot.

4 servings

prep 20 mins
• cook 15 mins

low fat

Chicken kiev

Make sure the chicken is thoroughly coated in egg and bread crumbs to prevent the butter from leaking out.

INGREDIENTS

8 tbsp butter, softened
2 garlic cloves, crushed through a press
2 tbsp chopped parsley
grated zest of 1 lemon
salt and freshly ground black pepper
4 boneless, skinless chicken breasts
3 tbsp all-purpose flour
1 large egg, beaten
1½ cups fresh bread crumbs
vegetable oil, for deep-frying

METHOD

1 Combine the butter, garlic, parsley, and lemon zest in a bowl. Season with salt and pepper. On a piece of plastic wrap, shape into a thick rectangle, then enclose in the plastic wrap. Refrigerate at least 1 hour, until firm.

2 One at a time, pound each breast between two sheets of plastic wrap with a meat pounder to an even thickness. Season the breasts. Cut the butter into 4 equal sticks and place a stick on each chicken breast. Fold in the sides, then roll up the chicken completely around the butter.

3 Roll each chicken packet in flour, then in beaten egg, and finally into the bread crumbs to coat evenly. Take care to keep the chicken closed around the butter.

4 Add enough oil to come halfway up the sides of a large saucepan and heat over high heat to 350°F (180°C). Add the chicken and cook about 5 minutes, until deep golden brown.

5 Transfer the cooked chicken to paper towels and drain briefly. Serve hot.

GOOD WITH A fresh mixed salad and sautéed potatoes.

PREPARE AHEAD The chicken can be prepared through step 3 and refrigerated for up to 1 day before frying.

4 servings

prep 25 mins, plus chilling time • cook 8–10 mins

Southern fried chicken

This is succulent comfort food from the Deep South, with the traditional accompaniment of a smooth cream gravy.

INGREDIENTS

$1^2/_3$ cups all-purpose flour
1 tsp dried thyme
1 tsp Cajun seasoning
1 tsp sugar
salt and freshly ground black pepper
4 chicken drumsticks
4 chicken thighs
2 large eggs
vegetable oil, for deep-frying

For the cream sauce

$1^1/_2$ tbsp all-purpose flour
$1^1/_4$ cups whole milk

METHOD

1 Combine the flour, thyme, Cajun seasoning, and sugar in the plastic food bag and season well with salt and pepper.

2 One at a time, add the drumsticks and thighs to the bag and shake until coated. Transfer to a wax paper-lined baking sheet.

3 Beat the eggs in a shallow dish. Dip the floured chicken in the egg, then return to the flour and coat again. Place the chicken on the baking sheet and chill for 30 minutes.

4 Fill the large deep saucepan halfway with oil and heat over high heat to 325°F (160°C). Add the chicken and deep-fry for about 20 minutes or until cooked through. Transfer to paper towels.

5 To make the cream gravy, transfer 2 tbsp of the frying oil to a saucepan. Whisk in the flour. Cook over low heat for 1 minute, then whisk in the milk. Cook, whisking often, until thickened. Season with salt and pepper.

GOOD WITH Mashed potatoes and corn on the cob.

PREPARE AHEAD Steps 1 and 2 can be completed 1 hour or more before cooking.

4 servings

**prep 20 mins,
plus chilling
• cook 25 mins**

**large self-sealing
plastic food bag,
large deep
saucepan,
deep-frying
thermometer**

Chicken breasts in garlic sauce

Don't be put off by the large quantity of garlic—the flavor mellows during cooking.

INGREDIENTS

15 garlic cloves, unpeeled
1 tbsp olive oil
1 tbsp butter
4 chicken breasts, with skin and bone
2 cups hard dry cider
1 cup apple juice
1 bay leaf
3/4 cup heavy cream
salt and freshly ground black pepper
1 tbsp chopped thyme

METHOD

1 Preheat the oven to 350°F (180°C). Parcook the unpeeled garlic cloves in boiling salted water for 4 minutes. Drain, rinse under cold running water, and peel. Set aside.

2 Heat the oil and butter in the casserole over medium-high heat. Add the chicken, skin side down, and cook for about 4 minutes, or until the skin is deep golden brown. Turn over, add the cider, apple juice, garlic cloves, and bay leaf, and bring to a simmer. Cover and bake for 20–25 minutes, or until the chicken shows no sign of pink when pierced with a knife.

3 Using a slotted spoon, transfer the chicken and half of the garlic to a deep platter and keep warm. Skim the fat from the cooking juices, then bring to a boil over high heat. Cook, crushing the garlic into the sauce with a spoon, about 5 minutes, or until thickened.

4 Add the cream and cook for 1 minute. Season with salt and pepper. Return the chicken to the casserole and baste. Sprinkle with the thyme and serve immediately.

GOOD WITH Boiled new potatoes and green beans.

4 servings

**prep 10 mins
• cook 40 mins**

**shallow flame-
proof casserole**

**freeze, without
the cream and
thyme, for up
to 3 months**

Thai green chicken curry

Use Thai curry paste, available at Asian markets and many supermarkets, to make this quick and flavorful dish.

INGREDIENTS

1 tbsp vegetable oil
4 skinless, boneless chicken breasts,
    about 5oz (140g) each,
    cut into bite-sized pieces
4 tsp Thai green or red curry paste
    (or more for a spicier sauce)
14fl oz (400ml) can coconut milk
2 tbsp soy sauce
4 large white button mushrooms,
    wiped and chopped
6 scallions, trimmed, green part only,
    cut into 1/4in (5mm) slices
salt and freshly ground black pepper
chopped cilantro, to garnish

METHOD

1 Heat the oil in a large frying pan over medium heat. Add the chicken and stir-fry for 2 minutes, or until browned. Stir in the curry paste.

2 Add the coconut milk and soy sauce, and bring to a boil, stirring often. Reduce the heat, and stir in the mushrooms, and most of the scallions. Simmer for about 8 minutes, or until the chicken is tender, and the juices run clear when pierced with the point of a knife. Season with salt and pepper to taste.

3 Serve hot, garnished with the cilantro and remaining scallions.

GOOD WITH A bowl of long-grain rice or plain noodles.

PREPARE AHEAD This dish can be cooked in advance and reheated.

4 servings

prep 10 mins • cook 10 mins

Chicken schnitzels

This quick dish works well for a family supper or dinner party.

INGREDIENTS
$\frac{1}{3}$ cup all-purpose flour
1 large egg
$\frac{1}{2}$ cup fine dry bread crumbs
4 skinless, boneless chicken breasts
salt and freshly ground black pepper
6 tbsp canola oil
4 lemon halves, to serve

METHOD
1 Spread the flour in a shallow bowl, beat the egg in another bowl, and spread the bread crumbs in a third bowl.

2 Put the chicken, and the thin, small fillets, if attached, between 2 sheets of waxed paper and pound with a rolling pin until they are about $\frac{1}{4}$ in (5mm) thick. Season with salt and pepper.

3 Coat the chicken one piece at a time, first in the flour, then in the beaten egg, and then in the bread crumbs, pressing them on to both sides. Refrigerate, uncovered, for at least 30 minutes. Preheat the oven to 200°F (95°C).

4 When ready to cook, heat 3 tbsp of the oil in a very large nonstick frying pan over medium-high heat until hot. Add 2 schnitzels to the pan and fry for 3 minutes on each side, until golden brown, and the juices run clear when pierced with the tip of a knife.

5 Drain the schnitzels well on paper towels, and keep warm in the oven. Heat the remaining oil in the pan, then add the remaining schnitzels, and fry as above. Serve with the lemon halves.

6 Serve immediately, garnished with lemon halves, for squeezing over the schnitzels.

GOOD WITH Sautéed potatoes and green beans. Leftovers are good eaten cold with a fresh potato salad.

PREPARE AHEAD The chicken can be prepared up to step 3, and then covered and refrigerated for up to 8 hours.

4 servings

**prep 10 mins, plus
30 mins chilling
• cook 12 mins**

**can be frozen
up to 3 months;
thaw, then
reheat in a 350°F
(180°C) oven**

Seared herbed chicken with green herb sauce

The crumb crust seals in juices, keeping the meat succulent.

INGREDIENTS

4 boneless and skinless chicken breasts
salt and freshly ground black pepper
$\frac{1}{2}$ cup all-purpose flour
$2\frac{1}{2}$ cups fresh bread crumbs
1 cup freshly grated Parmesan cheese
2 tbsp chopped thyme
2 tbsp chopped parsley
2 large eggs, lightly beaten
$\frac{1}{4}$ cup olive oil
$\frac{1}{4}$ cup vegetable oil

For the green herb sauce

1 large egg, plus 2 egg yolks
2 tbsp white wine vinegar
1 tbsp Dijon mustard
salt and freshly ground black pepper
$1\frac{1}{4}$ cups vegetable oil
2 tbsp chopped basil, dill, parsley, or chives

METHOD

1 For the sauce, combine the egg, yolks, vinegar, and mustard in a food processor. With the machine running, gradually add the oil to make a thick and creamy mayonnaise. Season with salt and pepper. Transfer to a bowl and stir in the basil.

2 Lightly pound the chicken breasts to an even thickness and season with salt and pepper. Spread the flour in a shallow dish. Mix the bread crumbs, Parmesan cheese, thyme, and parsley in a shallow bowl. Beat the eggs in another bowl. Coat the chicken in the flour, shaking off the excess. Dip in the eggs, then coat with the breadcrumb mixture.

3 Heat the olive and vegetable oils in a large frying pan over medium-high heat until shimmering. Add the chicken and cook, turning once, until golden brown, about 10 minutes. Transfer to paper towels to drain briefly. Serve hot with the sauce passed on the side.

4 servings

prep 20 mins
•cook 20–30 mins

freeze for up to 2 months

Sweet and sour chicken

This classic dish is one of the most popular of all Chinese-American culinary creations.

INGREDIENTS

4 skinless and boneless chicken breasts,
 cut into 1in (2.5cm) pieces
vegetable oil, for deep-frying
½ cup all-purpose flour
2 tbsp unsalted cashew nuts
 or whole blanched almonds
½ red bell pepper, seeded and chopped
8 scallions, cut into 1in (2.5cm) lengths
½ cup cubed fresh or drained canned pineapple

For the sauce
½ cup chicken stock
3 tbsp soy sauce
3 tbsp rice vinegar
2 tbsp ketchup
1 tbsp honey
one ¾in (2cm) piece fresh ginger,
 peeled and shredded
1 tsp cornstarch dissolved in 1 tbsp cold water

For the batter
¾ cup all-purpose flour
¾ tsp baking powder
⅛ tsp salt
1 cup lager beer

METHOD

1 To make the batter, sift the flour, baking powder, and salt into a large bowl. Make a well in the center, add ½ cup of the beer, and whisk, gradually adding the remaining beer. Let stand for 30 minutes.

2 To make the sauce, stir the stock, soy sauce, vinegar, ketchup, honey, and ginger in a small saucepan over low heat until the honey is melted. Stir in the dissolved cornstarch and bring to a simmer. Cook, stirring often, until just thickened. Set aside.

3 Preheat the oven to 200°F (95°C). Fill a wok halfway with oil. Heat to 350°F (180°C). Place the flour in a bowl. In batches, toss the chicken in the flour, then coat in the batter and add to the hot oil. Deep-fry about 3 minutes. Transfer the chicken to a baking sheet lined with paper towels and keep warm in the oven.

4 Pour all but 2 tbsp oil from the wok and return to high heat. Add the cashews and stir-fry for 30 seconds. Transfer to the baking sheet. Add the red pepper to the oil and stir-fry 2 minutes, or until crisp-tender. Add the scallions and pineapple and stir-fry for 1 minute.

5 Pour the sauce into the wok, add the chicken and stir until coated. Transfer to a serving platter, sprinkle with cashews, and serve hot.

PREPARE AHEAD Steps 1 and 2 can be completed several hours in advance.

4 servings

**prep 30 mins,
plus standing
• cook 25 mins**

**wok or large
frying pan,
deep-frying
thermometer**

Chicken with herb sauce

This punchy sauce for chicken is easy to make—just blend all the ingredients in a food processor.

INGREDIENTS
6 boneless and skinless chicken breasts
1 small onion, sliced
1 carrot, chopped
1 celery stalk, chopped
a few parsley sprigs

For the sauce
1/2 cup packed parsley leaves
1/2 cup packed basil leaves
1 tbsp nonpareil capers, rinsed
1 tbsp red wine vinegar
2 anchovy fillets in oil, drained
1 garlic clove, minced
1/2 cup olive oil
salt and freshly ground black pepper

METHOD
1 Preheat the oven to 375°F (190°C). Place the chicken in a roasting pan. Add the onion, carrot, celery, and parsley and enough water to cover. Cover with aluminum foil. Bake for 30 minutes. Remove from the oven, uncover, and let cool.

2 Pulse the parsley, basil, capers, vinegar, anchovies, and garlic in a food processor until combined. With the machine running, slowly pour in the oil. Season with salt and pepper.

3 Remove the chicken from the liquid and thinly slice across the grain. Transfer to a platter, top with the sauce, and serve.

GOOD WITH A selection of roasted vegetables, such as artichokes.

4 servings

prep 10 mins
• cook 30 mins

Turkey à la king

This dish is very easy to make and the sweet paprika adds a rich spiciness.

INGREDIENTS
2 tbsp vegetable oil
4 tbsp butter
1 onion, finely sliced
1 red bell pepper, seeded and chopped
1 green bell pepper, seeded and chopped
6oz (175g) white mushrooms, sliced
2 tbsp all-purpose flour
salt and freshly ground black pepper
2 cups whole milk, heated
3–4 cups diced cooked turkey
sweet paprika, for garnish

METHOD
1 Heat the oil and butter in a large pan over medium heat. Add the onion and red and green peppers and cook, stirring occasionally, until softened, about 5 minutes. Add the mushrooms and cook until they soften, about 5 minutes more.

2 Sprinkle in the flour. Stir in the milk and cook, stirring constantly, until the sauce is boiling and thickened. Season with salt and pepper to taste.

3 Stir in the turkey and simmer for about 5 minutes, stirring occasionally, until the turkey is heated through. Sprinkle with the paprika and serve hot.

GOOD WITH Steamed rice, mashed potatoes, or egg noodles.

PREPARE AHEAD The dish can be cooled, covered, and refrigerated up to 1 day ahead, then reheated gently before serving.

4 servings

prep 15 mins • cook 15 mins

freeze for up to 3 months; thaw completely before reheating

Devilled turkey

Serve these spicy stir-fried turkey strips as a healthy lunch or supper.

INGREDIENTS

2 tbsp olive oil
1lb (450g) turkey breast cutlets, cut into strips
1 onion, finely chopped
1 red bell pepper, seeded and cut into strips
1 orange bell pepper, seeded and cut into strips
1 garlic clove, minced
3 tbsp fresh orange juice
2 tbsp whole grain mustard
2 tbsp mango chutney
¼ tsp sweet paprika
2 tbsp Worcestershire sauce
1 fresh hot red chili, seeded and minced

METHOD

1 Heat the oil in a nonstick frying pan over a high heat. Add the turkey and cook, stirring often, about 5 minutes, until lightly browned. Transfer to a plate.

2 Add the onion and stir-fry about 2 minutes, or until it is just beginning to color. Add the red and orange peppers and garlic and stir-fry about 3 minutes.

3 Mix the orange juice, mustard, chutney, paprika, Worcestershire sauce, and chili together until well combined. Stir into the vegetables and return the turkey to the pan. Cook about 5 minutes or until piping hot and the turkey is opaque throughout. Serve hot.

GOOD WITH Stir-fried spinach and rice or noodles.

4 servings

prep 10 mins
• cook 15 mins

Chicken jalfrezi

This spicy chicken curry is made with chilies and mustard seeds.

INGREDIENTS

2 tbsp vegetable oil
2 tbsp garam masala
2 tsp ground cumin
2 tsp yellow mustard seeds
1 tsp ground turmeric
1 onion, sliced
1in (2.5cm) piece of fresh ginger,
    peeled and finely minced
3 garlic cloves, minced
1 red bell pepper, seeded and sliced
½ green bell pepper, seeded and sliced
2 fresh hot green chilies, seeded and finely minced
1½lb (675g) skinless and boneless chicken thighs or breasts,
    cut into 1in (2.5cm) pieces
1 cup canned chopped tomatoes
3 tbsp chopped cilantro

METHOD

1 Heat the oil in a large saucepan over a medium heat. Add the garam masala, cumin, mustard seeds, and turmeric, and stir for 1 minute, until fragrant.

2 Add the onion, ginger, and garlic, and cook, stirring often, for about 2 minutes, until the onion starts to soften. Add the peppers and the chilies and cook for 5 minutes, stirring often.

3 Increase the heat to medium-high. Add the chicken, and cook until it begins to brown. Add the tomatoes and cilantro, lower the heat, and simmer for 10 minutes, or until the chicken is cooked through, stirring frequently. Serve hot.

GOOD WITH Basmati rice.

PREPARE AHEAD The curry can be refrigerated for up to one day. Reheat, adding a little more stock, if needed.

4 servings

prep 20 mins
• cook 25 mins

low fat

freeze for up to
3 months

Turkey cutlets with artichokes

A delicious take on the classic veal dish, this features coated cutlets topped with a tomato and artichoke sauce.

INGREDIENTS
1/4 cup all-purpose flour
1/2 tsp each salt and freshly ground black pepper
4 turkey breast cutlets, about 4oz (115g) each
3 tbsp olive oil
1 small onion, finely chopped
1/4 cup dry white wine
one 6oz (170g) jar marinated artichoke hearts, drained
1 cup drained canned chopped tomatoes
few basil leaves, torn

METHOD
1 Combine the flour, salt, and pepper on a plate. Dip the turkey in the seasoned flour until lightly coated, shaking off any excess. Heat 1 tbsp of the oil in a large frying pan over medium heat. Add 2 of the cutlets and cook, turning once, 2–3 minutes each side, or just until golden brown and cooked through. Transfer to a platter and cover with aluminum foil to keep warm. Repeat the process with the remaining cutlets and 1 tbsp oil.

2 Add the remaining 1 tbsp oil to the pan and cook the onion for 4–5 minutes, or until softened. Add the wine and bring to a boil, stirring up the brown bits from the bottom of the pan. Stir in the artichokes, tomatoes, and basil and bring to a boil. Spoon over the cutlets and serve hot.

GOOD WITH Buttered fettuccine or other flat pasta noodles.

4 servings

prep 10 mins
• cook 20–25 mins

Garlicky turkey burgers

The epitome of fast food, these spicy burgers take no time to prepare and are an instant hearty supper.

INGREDIENTS
1lb (454g) ground turkey
1/3 cup fresh bread crumbs
2 tbsp finely chopped onion
2 tbsp chopped parsley
2 tsp Dijon mustard
2 garlic cloves, finely chopped
1 large egg white
1/2 tsp each salt and freshly ground black pepper
vegetable oil cooking spray
4 seeded buns, toasted
1 large ripe tomato, sliced
1 cup shredded lettuce

METHOD
1 Mix the turkey, bread crumbs, onion, parsley, pepper, mustard, garlic, egg white, and salt and pepper together in a bowl until well combined. Form into 4 burgers, each about 1cm (1/2in) thick.

2 Spray a large nonstick frying pan with the oil and heat over medium heat. Add the burgers and cook, turning once, about 8 minutes, until they spring back in the center when pressed. Place a turkey burger in each bun, top with the tomatoes and lettuce, and serve.

GOOD WITH Your favorite condiments and pickles.

4 servings

prep 10 mins
• cook 6 mins

Chinese-style lemon chicken

This is one of those dishes that was probably invented to appeal to Western diners, since lemons are rarely used in Chinese cooking.

INGREDIENTS

1¼ cups all-purpose flour
1 tsp baking powder
¼ tsp baking soda
¼ tsp salt
4 boneless chicken breasts
vegetable oil, for deep-frying
bok choy, steamed, to serve
hot cooked rice, to serve

For the lemon sauce

¼ cup fresh lemon juice
3 tbsp cornstarch
1½ cups chicken stock
2 tbsp honey
2 tbsp light brown sugar
one ½in (1cm) piece of fresh ginger,
   peeled and shredded

METHOD

1 Sift the flour, baking powder, baking soda, and salt into a large bowl, add 1¼ cups cold water and whisk until smooth. Set aside for 30 minutes.

2 Preheat the oven to 200°F (100°C). Line a baking sheet with paper towels. Add enough oil to come about halway up the sides of a heavy deep frying pan. Heat over high heat to 350°F (180°C) on a deep-frying thermometer. In batches, dip the chicken into the batter. Carefully add the oil and deep-fry, turning once, for 5–6 minutes, or until golden. Transfer to the baking sheet and keep warm in the oven.

3 Meanwhile, make the sauce. Pour the lemon juice into a medium saucepan, sprinkle in the cornstarch, and whisk until smooth. Add the stock, honey, sugar, and ginger. Stir over low heat until the sauce comes to a boil and thickens. Simmer for 1 minute.

4 Arrange the chicken on a serving platter and spoon the hot sauce over the top. Serve hot with the bok choy and rice.

PREPARE AHEAD The batter can be made a couple hours in advance.

4 servings

**prep 20 mins,
plus standing
• cook 30 mins**

**deep-frying
thermometer**

Couscous royale

This richly spiced dish makes a colorful Moroccan feast.

INGREDIENTS

2 tbsp olive oil
1lb 5oz (600g) boneless leg of lamb, cut into bite-sized chunks
6 chicken legs, about 3lb 3oz (1.5kg)
1 red bell pepper, seeded and diced
1 eggplant, cut into 1in (2.5cm) pieces
1 large red onion, sliced
2 garlic cloves, finely chopped
4 tsp harissa (hot Moroccan chili paste)
1 tbsp sweet paprika
1 tsp ground turmeric
2 medium zucchini, sliced
1 cup chicken stock
15oz (420g) can chickpeas, rinsed and drained
14.5oz (400g) can chopped tomatoes
6oz (175g) chorizo, thickly sliced
salt and freshly ground black pepper
large sprig of thyme
1 bay leaf
2$\frac{1}{4}$ cups couscous
chopped cilantro, to garnish

METHOD

1 Heat the oil in the casserole over medium-high heat. Add the lamb and chicken and cook, turning occasionally, about 6 minutes. Transfer to paper towels to drain.

2 Add the eggplant, red pepper, onion, and garlic to the casserole and cook, stirring occasionally, about 4 minutes. Stir in the harissa, paprika, and turmeric and cook for 1 minute.

3 Return the lamb and chicken to the casserole. Add the zucchini, stock, beans, tomatoes, and chorizo and season with salt and pepper. Bring to a boil. Reduce the heat to low and cover. Simmer about 1 hour, or until the meats are tender.

4 Strain the mixture in a colander set over a wide skillet. Transfer the meat and vegetables to a platter and cover to keep warm. Boil the strained liquid over high heat for about 5 minutes, or until slightly reduced. Season with salt and pepper.

5 Bring 3 cups water and $\frac{1}{2}$ tsp salt to a boil in a large saucepan. Stir in the couscous and remove from the heat. Cover and let stand until the couscous is tender, about 5 minutes. Stir the meats and vegetables into the couscous. Pour the sauce on top and sprinkle with the cilantro. Serve hot.

6 servings

prep 10 mins
• cook 1 hr
20 mins

large flame-
proof casserole

freeze for up to
1 month

Chicken piri-piri

Portugal's favorite chicken is hot and spicy.

INGREDIENTS

1 chicken, about 3½lb (1.6kg)
6 fresh hot red or green chilies
½ cup olive oil
¼ cup red wine vinegar
2 tsp hot paprika
½ tsp dried oregano
3 garlic cloves
1 tsp salt

METHOD

1 Preheat the oven to 375°F (190°C). Spread the chilies on a baking sheet. Roast about 15 minutes, until shriveled. Let cool, then remove the stalks from the chilies. Combine the whole chilies, oil, vinegar, paprika, oregano, garlic, and salt in a saucepan. Simmer over low heat for about 3 minutes. Let cool. Purée in a blender.

2 To butterfly the chicken, use kitchen shears to remove the backbone of the chicken. Press down on the breastbone to spread out the chicken (see page 16). Transfer the chicken to a nonreactive dish. Coat the chicken with the marinade. Cover and refrigerate for at least 1 hour.

3 Preheat the oven to 400°F (200°C). Remove the chicken from the marinade and place on a baking sheet, skin side up. Roast about 1 hour. Serve hot.

GOOD WITH Boiled or steamed rice, guacamole, and a simple salad.

4 servings

prep 20 mins,
plus cooling
and marinating
• cook 1 hr 15
mins

94

ONE-POT

Jambalaya

This one-pot meal captures the spicy flavors of Louisiana.

INGREDIENTS

4 tbsp rendered bacon fat or vegetable oil

4 skinless and boneless chicken thighs,
    cut into bite-sized pieces

8oz (225g) andouille or kielbasa sausage, thickly sliced

1 onion, finely chopped

1 red bell pepper, seeded
    and finely chopped

1 green bell pepper, seeded and finely chopped

1 celery stalk, thinly sliced

2 garlic cloves, finely chopped

1 fresh hot red chili, seeded
    and chopped

1¾ cups long-grain rice

2 tbsp tomato paste

2 tsp dried thyme

1 tsp salt

½ tsp sweet paprika

¼ tsp cayenne pepper

2 bay leaves

pinch of sugar

freshly ground black pepper

2½ cups chicken or
    vegetable stock

one 14.5oz (411g) can chopped
    tomatoes

1 tsp Worcestershire sauce

12 large shrimp, peeled
    and deveined

chopped parsley, to garnish

hot red pepper sauce, to serve

METHOD

1 Heat 2 tbsp of the bacon fat in the casserole over high heat. In batches, add the chicken. Cook, stirring occasionally, for 10 minutes, or until the chicken is browned and opaque throughout. Using a slotted spoon, transfer the chicken to a plate.

2 Add the remaining bacon fat to the casserole and heat. Add the andouille and cook, stirring occasionally, for 5 minutes, or until browned. Remove the andouille with a slotted spoon and set aside with the chicken.

3 Add the onion, peppers, celery, garlic, and chili to the casserole. Cook, stirring often, for 5 minutes or until softened. Add the rice and cook, stirring often, for about 3 minutes. Add the tomato paste and stir for another minute.

4 Return the chicken and sausage to the casserole. Add the thyme, salt, paprika, cayenne, bay leaves, sugar, and pepper. Pour in the stock, the tomatoes with their juice, and the Worcestershire sauce. Bring to the boil over medium-high heat, stirring often. Reduce the heat to low and cover. Simmer for 12–15 minutes, or until the peppers are tender.

5 Add the shrimp and simmer, still covered, for 3–5 minutes, or until the rice is tender and the shrimp are pink (the jambalaya should be a little soupy). Transfer to a serving bowl and garnish with parsley. Serve hot, with a bottle of hot pepper sauce alongside.

GOOD WITH Cold beer to quell the spiciness.

4–6 servings

prep 30 mins
• cook 45 mins

large
flame-proof
casserole

Chicken pot pie

This is a great recipe for transforming leftover roast chicken into a satisfying family meal.

INGREDIENTS

2½ cups hot chicken stock
2 carrots, peeled and sliced
2 parsnips, peeled and sliced
2 tbsp butter
1 onion, finely chopped
2 celery stalks, thinly sliced
2 tbsp all-purpose flour
10oz (300g) frozen fava or lima beans, or peas, thawed
½ tsp dry mustard
salt and freshly ground black pepper
12oz (350g) skinless, boneless cooked chicken, cut into bite-sized pieces
1 cup heavy cream
1 sheet (8½oz/240g) frozen puff pastry, thawed
1 large egg, beaten, to glaze

METHOD

1 Put the stock, carrots, and parsnips in a large saucepan over high heat and bring to a boil. Cook for 5 minutes or until the vegetables are crisp-tender. Strain in a sieve over a bowl, and reserve the stock and vegetables.

2 Melt the butter in another saucepan over medium heat. Add the onion and celery, and cook, stirring often, for 5 minutes or until softened. Sprinkle in the flour and stir for 1 minute.

3 Gradually stir in the reserved stock and bring to a boil, stirring. Reduce the heat and simmer for 2 minutes. Stir in the fava beans and mustard, and season with salt and pepper. Remove from the heat and cool until tepid. Stir in the chicken, cream, and reserved vegetables. Pour into the pie pan.

4 Preheat the oven to 400°F (200°C). Roll out the pastry on a lightly floured surface until about ⅛in (3mm) thick. Cut out a round of dough slightly larger than the dish. Brush the dish rim with water, then position the pastry over the filling, and fold over the excess pastry so the dough is double-thick around the circumference of the pan. Crimp the pastry, glaze the top with the some beaten egg, and cut a small hole in the top.

5 Place the pie on a baking sheet. Bake for 25 minutes or until the pastry is puffed and golden, and the filling is hot. Let cool for a few minutes, then serve.

GOOD WITH Steamed broccoli and, for heartier appetites, some boiled new potatoes.

PREPARE AHEAD The pie can be assembled a day in advance, refrigerated, and then baked in the preheated oven.

4 servings

prep 15 mins
• cook 25 mins

9.5in (24cm)
deep-dish
pie pan

the pie filling
can be left to
cool completely,
and then frozen
after step 3; do
not refreeze if
the cooked
chicken has
previously
been frozen

Chicken and apricot tagine

The dried fruit and warm spices in this dish are the unmistakable flavors of the Middle East.

INGREDIENTS

2 tbsp vegetable oil
1 onion, finely chopped
1 garlic clove, finely chopped
1 tsp ground ginger
1 tsp ground cumin
1 tsp ground turmeric
pinch of ground cinnamon
pinch of crushed hot red pepper
2$\frac{1}{2}$ cups chicken stock
1 tbsp tomato paste
8oz (225g) mixed dried fruit, such as apricots
    and raisins, chopped if large
$\frac{1}{4}$ cup fresh orange juice
salt and freshly ground black pepper
1$\frac{1}{2}$lb (675g) skinless, boneless chicken breasts,
    cut into bite-sized chunks
2 tbsp chopped cilantro, to garnish

METHOD

1 Heat the oil in the casserole over medium heat. Add the onion, garlic, ground spices, and hot red pepper. Cook, stirring, for 5 minutes or until the onions are softened. Stir in the stock and tomato paste, and bring to a boil, stirring.

2 Add the dried fruits and orange juice. Season with salt and pepper. Reduce the heat, partially cover, and simmer for 15 minutes or until the fruits have softened and the juices reduced slightly.

3 Add the chicken and re-cover the casserole. Simmer for 20 minutes or until the juices run clear. Adjust the seasoning, if necessary. Sprinkle with cilantro and serve hot.

GOOD WITH Couscous, which is the traditional accompaniment.

PREPARE AHEAD The tagine can be cooked in advance, left to cool, and refrigerated for up to 2 days.

4 servings

**prep 15 mins
• cook 35 mins**

**large
flame-proof
casserole**

Chicken korma

A mild curry popular in Indian restaurants, this is a fragrant and aromatic dish with a creamy sauce.

INGREDIENTS

4 tbsp vegetable oil or ghee
8 boneless and skinless chicken thighs,
    cut into 1in (2½cm) pieces
2 large onions, thinly sliced
2 garlic cloves, crushed
1 tbsp ground coriander
1 tbsp ground cumin
1 tsp ground turmeric
1 tsp chili powder
1 tsp ground cardamom
½ tsp ground ginger
⅔ cup low-fat plain yogurt
1 tbsp cornstarch
1¼ cups chicken stock
⅔ cup heavy cream
1 tbsp fresh lemon juice

METHOD

1 Heat 2 tbsp of the oil in a large frying pan over medium-high heat. In batches, add the chicken and cook, stirring occasionally, for about 5 minutes, until browned. Transfer to a plate.

2 Add the remaining 2 tbsp oil to the pan and reduce the heat to medium. Add the onions and garlic and cook, stirring often, about 5 minutes, until golden. Add the coriander, cumin, turmeric, chili powder, cardamom, and ginger and reduce the heat to low. Cook, stirring often, about 2 minutes, or until the spices are fragrant.

3 Mix the yogurt and cornstarch together, then stir into the pan. Stir in the remaining stock. Bring to a boil, stirring constantly. Return the chicken to the pan and simmer, stirring occasionally, for 15 minutes, or until the chicken is opaque.

4 Stir in the cream and lemon juice and simmer for 5 minutes more. Serve hot.

GOOD WITH Herb-flecked rice.

4 servings

prep 20 mins
• cook 45 mins

freeze for up to
1 month

Chicken cacciatore

This Italian dish translates as "hunter-style chicken," and is traditionally served with polenta to soak up the delicious juices.

INGREDIENTS

4 chicken legs, about 3lb 3oz (1.5kg) total weight
salt and freshly ground black pepper
2 tbsp olive oil
1 onion, chopped
2 garlic cloves, sliced
$^3/_4$ cup dry white wine
one 14.5oz (411g) can chopped tomatoes
$^2/_3$ cup chicken stock
7oz (200g) white mushrooms, sliced
1 celery stalk, chopped
1 tbsp tomato paste
2 tsp chopped rosemary
2 tsp chopped sage
8 pitted Kalamata olives, halved

METHOD

1 Trim any excess fat from the chicken and season them with salt and pepper. Heat 1 tbsp of the oil in the casserole over medium-high heat. In batches, add the chicken and cook, turning once, for about 4 minutes, until browned. Transfer to a plate. Pour the fat out of the pan.

2 Add the remaining 1 tbsp oil and heat over medium-low heat. Add the onion and garlic and cook, stirring often, about 3 minutes, until softened. Stir in the wine and boil for 1 minute, scraping up the browned bits in the pan. Stir in the tomatoes, stock, mushrooms, celery, tomato paste, rosemary, and sage and bring to a simmer.

3 Return the chicken to the pan and cover. Simmer for 40 minutes, or until the chicken shows no sign of pink when pierced at the bone. During the last 10 minutes, add the olives. Serve hot.

GOOD WITH Soft polenta or pasta and a mixed green salad.

4 servings

prep 20 mins
• cook 35–40 mins

low fat

large
flame-proof
casserole

Chicken tikka masala

This creamy Indian dish gets extra flavor from its marinade.

INGREDIENTS

8 skinless and boneless chicken thighs
2 garlic cloves
1in (2.5cm) piece fresh ginger, peeled and sliced
2 tbsp fresh lime juice
1 fresh hot red chili, seeded
2 tbsp chopped cilantro, plus more to garnish
2 tbsp vegetable oil
1 red onion, chopped
1 tsp ground turmeric
1 tsp ground cumin
1¼ cups heavy cream
1 tbsp tomato paste
1 tbsp fresh lemon juice
salt and freshly ground black pepper

METHOD

1 Place the chicken thighs in a single layer in a shallow dish. Purée the garlic, ginger, lime juice, chili, cilantro, and 1 tbsp of the oil in a food processor. Spread over the chicken. Cover and refrigerate for at least 2 and up to 8 hours.

2 Heat the remaining oil over medium-high heat. Add the onion and cook about 4 minutes, until beginning to brown. Stir in the turmeric and cumin and cook for 30 seconds. Remove from the heat.

3 Preheat the broiler. Line the broiler rack with oiled aluminum foil. Remove the chicken from the marinade, reserving the marinade. Place on the rack and broil, turning occasionally, about 5 minutes, until the chicken is singed and almost cooked through.

4 Meanwhile, add the reserved marinade to the onion mixture. Stir in the cream, tomato paste, and lemon juice. Bring to a boil over high heat, stirring often. Add the chicken to the sauce and reduce the heat to medium. Simmer for 5 minutes, until the chicken is cooked through. Season with salt and pepper. Sprinkle with cilantro and serve hot.

GOOD WITH Pilau rice or warm naan bread.

PREPARE AHEAD The dish can be made 1 day in advance, allowed to cool, covered, and chilled until needed. Reheat gently before serving.

4 servings

prep 20 mins,
plus marinating
• cook 25 mins

freeze for up to
3 months

Chicken with chorizo

Inspired by Spanish cuisine, this is sure to become a favorite chicken dish.

INGREDIENTS

3 tbsp olive oil
4 chicken legs
salt and freshly ground black pepper
9oz (250g) smoked chorizo,
   cut into bite-sized pieces
1 red onion, thinly sliced
1 tsp ground coriander
1 red bell pepper, seeded and chopped
1 yellow bell pepper, seeded and chopped
1 large zucchini, sliced
2 garlic cloves, minced
1 tsp dried thyme
one 14.5oz (411g) can chopped tomatoes
1 cup chicken stock
$\frac{1}{4}$ cup dry sherry

METHOD

1 Preheat the oven to 350°F (180°C). Heat the oil in a large flameproof casserole over medium-high heat. Season the chicken with salt and pepper. Add the chicken and cook, turning occasionally, about 6 minutes, until browned; remove.

2 Add the chorizo to the casserole and cook, stirring often, for about 3 minutes; remove. Reduce the heat to medium-low and add the onion. Cook, about 5 minutes, or until softened. Add the coriander and stir for 1 minute. Add the peppers, zucchini, garlic, and thyme, and cook about 5 minutes, or until the peppers begin to soften.

3 Add the tomatoes, stock, and sherry and bring to a boil. Return the chicken and chorizo to the casserole, cover, and bake 40 minutes, or until the chicken is tender.

4 servings

prep 10 mins
• cook 1 hr
10 mins

freeze for up
to 1 month

Coq au vin

This French classic is perfect for entertaining.

INGREDIENTS

1 chicken, cut into 8 pieces
2 tbsp all-purpose flour
salt and freshly ground black pepper
4 tbsp butter
4oz (115g) pancetta, diced
1 carrot, diced
1 celery stalk, chopped
2 garlic cloves, minced
one 750ml bottle Pinot Noir
¼ cup brandy or Cognac
4 sprigs thyme
1 bay leaf
1 tbsp olive oil
1lb (450g) white boiling onions, peeled
1 tsp brown sugar
1 tsp red wine vinegar
8oz (225g) small white mushrooms

METHOD

1 Sprinkle the chicken with 1 tbsp of the flour and season with salt and pepper. Melt 2 tbsp of the butter in the casserole over medium heat. In batches, add the chicken and cook about 6 minutes, turning, until golden brown on all sides. Transfer to a plate.

2 Add the pancetta, carrot, celery, and garlic and cook about 5 minutes, until softened. Sprinkle in the remaining flour, stir well, and cook for 1 minute. Add the wine and brandy and bring to a boil, stirring up the browned bits in the pan. Return the chicken to the pan and add the thyme and bay leaf. Cover, reduce the heat to medium-low, and simmer about 30 minutes.

3 Meanwhile, melt the remaining butter with the oil in a frying pan over medium heat. Add the onions and cook about 6 minutes, until lightly browned. Stir in the sugar, vinegar, and 1 tbsp water. Add the onions and mushrooms to the chicken. Cook until the chicken is cooked through, about another 15 minutes.

4 Transfer the chicken and vegetables to a deep platter and keep warm. Discard the thyme and bay leaf. Skim off the fat from the surface of the sauce. Bring to a boil over high heat and cook for about 5 minutes, until the sauce thickens. Season with salt and pepper. Pour over the chicken and serve hot.

GOOD WITH Mashed potatoes and French beans.

PREPARE AHEAD You can make this dish 1 day in advance. Cover and chill until needed.

4 servings

**prep 30 mins
• cook 1 hr**

large flame-proof casserole

freeze for up to 3 months

Duck confit

For this classic French dish, look for duck fat online or render duck skin and fat purchased at an Asian butcher.

INGREDIENTS

4 duck legs
1 cup kosher or sea salt
4 garlic cloves, peeled and crushed
1 tbsp whole white peppercorns
1 tsp coriander seeds
5 juniper berries
1 tbsp chopped thyme
2¼lb (1kg) duck fat, melted

METHOD

1 Dry the duck legs on paper towels. Process the salt, garlic, peppercorns, coriander seeds, juniper berries, and thyme in a food processor until a rough paste forms. Transfer to a glass or ceramic baking dish. Add the duck legs, and rub with and bury in the salt mixture. Cover with plastic wrap and refrigerate for 12 hours.

2 Preheat the oven to 275°F (140°C). Rinse the duck well and pat dry. Transfer to a baking dish just large enough to hold the duck in a single layer, and add the duck fat.

3 Cook the duck for 1½ hours, or until very tender when tested with the tip of a knife.

4 Remove from the oven and let the duck cool completely in the fat. Transfer the confit and the fat to a zippered plastic bag and refrigerate for up to 5 days or freeze for up to 3 months.

5 When ready to serve, heat the duck with a thin layer of clinging fat in a skillet over medium heat, turning occasionally, about 12 minutes, until browned and heated through. Serve immediately.

GOOD WITH Mesclun salad and roasted root vegetables.

PREPARE AHEAD Make the confit up to 4 weeks in advance. Keep in the refrigerator until needed. To give you plenty of time, start the confit at least 1 day before you plan to serve it.

4 servings

prep 15 mins, plus chilling and curing • cook 1½ hrs

oven-proof baking dish

freeze for up to 6 months

Baked poussin with lemon and paprika

This meltingly succulent dish gets its subtle flavors from a blend of Egyptian and Spanish influences.

INGREDIENTS

4 lemons
4 large ripe tomatoes, peeled, seeded, and chopped
1 large onion, finely chopped
1 tbsp sweet paprika
2 tsp honey
4 bay leaves
salt
cayenne pepper
4 poussins
8 garlic cloves
1 tsp balsamic vinegar
lemon wedges and bay leaves, to garnish

METHOD

1 Preheat the oven to 400°F (200°C). Cut 2 lemons in half lengthwise, and then into thick slices. Combine the tomatoes, onion, lemon slices, paprika, honey, and bay leaves in a large ovenproof casserole with a lid. Season with the salt and cayenne.

2 Cut the 2 remaining lemons into quarters. Insert 2 lemon quarters and 2 garlic cloves into the cavity of each poussin. Arrange the poussins on the tomato mixture and season with salt.

3 Cover the casserole. Bake for 30 minutes. Uncover and reduce the oven temperature to 350°F (180°C) for 15 minutes more, or until the juices run clear when pierced in the thigh with the tip of a knife. Transfer the poussins to a platter and keep warm.

4 Skim the fat from the tomato mixture and discard the lemon slices and bay leaves. Purée the tomato mixture and balsamic vinegar in a food processor. Taste and adjust the seasoning. Serve the poussins hot, with the sauce.

4 servings

**prep 15 mins
• cook 45 mins**

low fat

**freeze for up to
2 months**

Creamy tarragon chicken

Fresh tarragon and cream is a classic pairing in French cuisine.

INGREDIENTS

2 tbsp butter

1 tbsp canola oil

4 chicken breasts, with skin and bones

9oz (250g) shallots, sliced

1 tsp dried *herbes de Provence*

2 garlic cloves, finely chopped

salt and freshly ground black pepper

1 cup hot chicken stock

½ cup dry white wine

1 cup crème fraîche

2 tbsp chopped tarragon,
   plus extra sprigs to garnish

METHOD

1 Melt the butter with the oil in the casserole over medium-high heat. Add the chicken breasts, skin sides down, and cook for 3 minutes, or until golden brown. Turn them over and brown the other sides, about 2 minutes more.

2 Turn the chicken breasts skin sides up, then sprinkle with the shallots, *herbes de Provence*, garlic, and salt and pepper to taste. Add the stock and wine and bring to a boil. Reduce the heat to low, cover the casserole, and simmer for 25 minutes, or until the chicken is tender and the juices run clear when pierced with the tip of a knife. Transfer the chicken to a platter and tent with aluminum foil. Boil the sauce over high heat until reduced by about half.

3 Stir in the crème fraîche and chopped tarragon and continue boiling until thickened. If the sauce becomes too thick, add more chicken stock; then adjust the seasoning, if necessary. Coat the chicken with the sauce, garnish with the tarragon, and serve hot.

GOOD WITH Boiled long-grain rice, or try mashed potatoes with olive oil, and chopped pitted black olives.

PREPARE AHEAD Steps 1 and 2 can be prepared up to 1 day in advance and kept in a covered container in the refrigerator. Reheat and make sure the chicken is completely heated through before stirring in the crème fraîche.

4 servings

prep 10 mins
• cook 35 mins

large flame-
proof casserole

the dish can be
left to cool
completely after
step 2, then
frozen for up
to 1 month;
thaw at room
temperature,
then complete
the recipe

Chicken with pancetta

Pancetta and chicken make a winning combination. Add the olives and capers for a delicious dish packed with Mediterranean flavors.

INGREDIENTS

8oz (225g) pancetta, diced
4 tbsp olive oil
4 garlic cloves, chopped
6 chicken breasts
salt and freshly ground black pepper
3 tbsp all-purpose flour
$1/4$ cup capers, rinsed and drained
2 tbsp white wine vinegar
12 pitted and chopped Kalamata olives
1 tbsp chopped thyme
$1/2$ cup heavy cream

METHOD

1 Cook the pancetta in the oil over medium heat until browned, about 7 minutes. Add the garlic and cook 1 minute. Transfer to a plate, leaving the fat in the pan.

2 Dust the chicken with flour, salt, and pepper. In batches, brown chicken in the pan fat about 5 minutes. Stir in the pancetta, capers, vinegar, olives, and thyme. Cover and simmer about 35 minutes, until cooked through. Transfer to a platter.

3 Add the cream to the pan and boil about 3 minutes, until thickened. Season. Pour over the chicken and serve hot.

6 servings

prep 15 mins
• cook 45 mins

Chicken in balsamic vinegar

This cold chicken dish has a lovely hint of sweetness from the balsamic vinegar and raisins.

INGREDIENTS

4 boneless and skinless chicken breasts
salt and freshly ground black pepper
1 cup dry white wine
1 cup extra virgin olive oil
¼ cup balsamic vinegar
¼ cup raisins, plumped up in boiling water
    for 10 mins and drained
1 tbsp chopped basil or tarragon
zest of 1 lemon
assorted mixed greens, such as arugula
    and watercress, to serve
½ cup pine nuts, toasted, to serve
lemon wedges, to serve

METHOD

1 Preheat the oven to 375°F (190°C). Using a flat meat pounder, lightly pound the chicken breasts between 2 sheets of plastic wrap to an even thickness. Place the chicken in a lightly oiled shallow roasting pan. Season with salt and pepper, then pour the wine over the chicken. Cover with a piece of parchment paper cut to fit inside of the pan. Bake for about 20 minutes, or until the chicken is opaque when pierced with a knife. Uncover the chicken, reserve 2 tbsp of the pan juices, and let the chicken and pan juices cool.

2 Whisk together the oil and vinegar in a small bowl, then whisk in the reserved pan juices. Add the raisins, basil, and lemon zest. Arrange the chicken in a nonmetallic dish. Pour the dressing over the chicken and cover with plastic wrap. Refrigerate, turning the chicken at least once in the dressing, for at least 12 hours and up to 24 hours.

3 Remove from the refrigerator 1 hour before serving. Arrange the mixed greens on a serving platter. Thinly slice the chicken, and place on the greens. Sprinkle with the pine nuts and garnish with the lemon wedges. Serve at once.

GOOD WITH Roasted cherry tomatoes on the vine, and hot, buttered new potatoes.

6 servings

prep 50 mins,
plus overnight
marinating
• cook 20 mins

Indian garlic chicken

Based on a classic Indian dish called *Murg Massalam*, this recipe can be roasted, broiled, or grilled.

INGREDIENTS

1 chicken, about 3¾lb (1.75kg),
    cut into 8 pieces, skin removed

For the marinade

¼ cup plain low-fat yogurt
2 tbsp fresh lemon juice
1 tbsp honey
2 garlic cloves, finely chopped
1 tsp salt
1 tsp ground ginger
½ tsp ground cardamom
½ tsp ground coriander
¼ tsp ground cumin
¼ tsp ground turmeric

METHOD

1 With a sharp knife, make a few shallow slashes in the chicken flesh and place in a nonmetallic dish.

2 To make the marinade, mix all the ingredients in a small bowl. Pour over the chicken, and toss until well coated. Cover and refrigerate for at least 1 hour and up to 1 day.

3 Preheat the oven to 400°F (200°C). Line a deep roasting pan with foil. Arrange the chicken in the pan. Pour about ⅔ cup water into the pan to form a shallow layer. Spoon any remaining marinade over the chicken. Bake for about 45 minutes, or until the chicken pieces are golden and crisp and show no sign of pink when pierced at the bone. Serve hot or cold.

GOOD WITH Basmati rice, flavored with a cinnamon stick and a few cardamom pods, a green salad, and naan bread.

4 servings

prep 10 mins, plus marinating • cook 1 hr

freeze for up to 1 month

Duck breasts with mushroom sauce

Special enough to serve to dinner guests, this recipe is surprisingly quick and easy.

INGREDIENTS

4 boneless duck breasts,
 about 7oz (200g) each
salt and freshly ground black pepper
2 tbsp olive oil
6oz (175g) white mushrooms,
 halved or quartered
4 scallions, chopped
1 tbsp fresh lemon juice
1 tbsp sun-dried tomato paste
1 tsp cornstarch
1¼ cups chicken stock
2 tbsp chopped parsley
3 tbsp white wine

METHOD

1 Score the duck skin with a thin sharp knife. Season the breasts with salt and pepper.

2 Heat the oil in a large frying pan over medium heat. Add the mushrooms and scallions and cook, stirring often, about 5 minutes, until the mushrooms are tender. Stir in the lemon juice and tomato paste.

3 Dissolve the cornstarch in ¼ cup of the stock and return to the remaining stock. Stir into the mushroom mixture. Bring to a boil, stirring often, until simmering and thickened. Stir in the parsley and season with salt and pepper. Remove the sauce from heat and keep warm.

4 Heat the grill pan over medium-high heat. Add the duck, skin side down. Cook until the skin is golden brown, pouring off the fat as needed, about 8 minutes. Turn and cook about 2 minutes more, until the duck is medium-rare.

5 Place the duck on a platter and tent with aluminum foil. Pour off any fat in the pan. Return to medium-high heat. Add the wine and stir to release any browned bits in the pan. Stir into the sauce.

6 Slice the duck and transfer to dinner plates. Top with the sauce, and serve hot.

GOOD WITH Boiled new potatoes and asparagus.

4 servings

prep 20 mins
• cook 25 mins

ridged cast-iron
grill pan

Duck with shallot confit

The spices and melted honey lend comforting winter flavors to the duck.

INGREDIENTS

6 duck breasts
1 tbsp honey
$\frac{1}{2}$ tsp Asian five-spice powder
salt and freshly ground black pepper

For the shallot confit

8oz (225g) shallots, peeled and thickly sliced
$\frac{2}{3}$ cup honey
2 tbsp peeled and minced fresh ginger
$\frac{2}{3}$ cup red wine vinegar

METHOD

1 To make the confit, combine the shallots, honey, and ginger in a saucepan. Cook over medium heat, stirring often, until the shallots are pale.

2 Stir in the vinegar and bring to a boil. Reduce the heat to medium-low and simmer for about 8 minutes, or until the liquid is syrupy. Stir in $\frac{2}{3}$ cup of water and simmer for about 8 minutes more, or until the mixture is golden and thickened, but not runny.

3 Meanwhile, preheat the oven to 400°F (200°C). Score the duck skin in a crosshatch pattern. Heat a large frying pan over medium-high heat. In batches, add the duck breasts, skin side down, and cook about 4 minutes, until the skin is browned, pouring off the fat as needed. Turn and cook the other side 2 minutes, until browned. Transfer to a roasting pan, skin side up. Brush with honey, sprinkle with the five-spice powder and salt and pepper. Bake for about 8 minutes, or until the duck breasts are medium-rare when pierced in the center.

4 Transfer to a carving board and let stand for 5 minutes. Carve on the diagonal into thick slices, transfer to dinner plates, and serve with the confit.

GOOD WITH A sweet potato purée, sautéed bok choy, or green beans with sesame seeds.

PREPARE AHEAD The shallot confit can be covered and refrigerated for up to 3 days.

6 servings

prep 10 mins
• cook 30 mins

Chicken biryani

For special occasions, this subtly spiced, aromatic dish from India is often decorated with small pieces of edible silver leaf.

INGREDIENTS
2 tbsp vegetable oil
2 tbsp butter
1 large onion, thinly sliced
2 garlic cloves, crushed and peeled
one 3in (7.5cm) cinnamon stick,
    broken into 2 or 3 pieces
6 cardamom pods
6 curry leaves (optional)
3 tbsp curry powder
1 tsp ground turmeric
$\frac{1}{2}$ tsp ground cumin
4 boneless and skinless chicken breasts,
    cut into 1in (2.5cm) pieces
$1\frac{1}{2}$ cups basmati rice
$\frac{1}{2}$ cup golden raisins
$3\frac{3}{4}$ cups chicken stock, as needed
2 tbsp toasted sliced almonds

METHOD
1 Heat the oil and butter in a large flameproof casserole over medium heat. Add the onion and garlic and cook, stirring often, about 4 minutes, until translucent. Add the cinnamon, cardamom pods, and curry leaves, if using, and cook, stirring often, for 5 minutes, until fragrant.

2 Add the curry powder, turmeric, and cumin, and stir for 1 minute. Add the chicken.

3 Add the rice and raisins and stir well. Pour in enough stock to just cover the rice. Bring to a boil. Reduce the heat to medium-low and cover. Simmer about 15 minutes or until the rice is tender and has absorbed the stock, adding more stock if the mixture becomes dry.

4 Transfer to a serving dish, fluffing the rice with a fork. Sprinkle with almonds and serve hot.

PREPARE AHEAD The biryani can be cooled, covered, and refrigerated for up to 1 day. Pour a few tablespoons of melted butter over it, cover, and bake in a 350°F (180°C) oven about 30 minutes.

4 servings

prep 20 mins
• cook 30 mins

low fat

Tandoori chicken

As tender and flavorful as the classic restaurant dish, this at-home recipe has a more natural color.

INGREDIENTS

4 chicken legs, skin removed
vegetable oil, for the broiler rack
4 tbsp butter, melted
1 red onion, thinly sliced, to serve
lemon wedges, to serve

For the tandoori marinade

1 onion, coarsely chopped
2 large garlic cloves, crushed and peeled
one $\frac{1}{2}$in (13mm) piece fresh ginger, peeled and coarsely chopped
3 tbsp fresh lemon juice
$1\frac{1}{4}$ tsp chili powder, to taste
1 tsp garam masala
$\frac{1}{4}$ tsp salt
pinch of ground turmeric
pinch of hot paprika
pinch of saffron threads

METHOD

1 To make the marinade, purée the onion, garlic, and ginger in a blender or food processor. Add the lemon juice, chili powder, garam masala, salt, turmeric, paprika, and saffron and process to combine.

2 Place the chicken legs in a nonmetallic bowl and pierce all over with a fork. Add the marinade and mix well. Cover with plastic wrap. Refrigerate for at least 3 hours, occasionally turning the pieces.

3 Preheat the oven to 425°F (220°C). Line a roasting pan with aluminum foil. Place a broiler rack over the pan and oil the rack. Remove the chicken from the marinade, and arrange on the rack. Brush with half of the melted butter.

4 Roast for about 25 minutes, or until the chicken is cooked through and the juices run clear when pierced with the tip of a knife.

5 Remove the pan from the oven. Preheat the broiler. Pour off the juices that have accumulated in the pan. Brush the chicken with more butter. Broil the chicken, still on the rack and pan, about 8in (20cm) from the source of heat for about 5 minutes, until the edges of the chicken are lightly charred. Serve hot, with the onions and lemon wedges.

PREPARE AHEAD The chicken can be marinated in the refrigerator for up to 24 hours.

4 servings

prep 10–15 mins, plus at least 3 hrs marinating • cook 25–35 mins

Chicken wrapped in pancetta and sage

This is a light but elegant main course to which you can add grilled peppers and olives.

INGREDIENTS

12 small plum tomatoes, halved
3 tbsp olive oil, plus more to drizzle
salt and freshly ground black pepper
3 skinless and boneless chicken breasts
12 sage leaves
12 slices of pancetta, unrolled
6oz (170g) mixed baby greens

For the dressing

$\frac{1}{3}$ cup olive oil
$1\frac{1}{2}$ tbsp cider vinegar
2 tsp chopped parsley
1 shallot, finely chopped
1 tsp light brown sugar
salt and freshly ground black pepper

METHOD

1 Preheat the oven to 300°F (150°C). Put the tomatoes into a roasting pan, drizzle with olive oil, and season with salt and pepper. Roast in the oven for 1 hour, or until slightly dried and caramelized.

2 To make the dressing, place the ingredients in a small bowl and whisk together until thickened slightly. Season to taste with salt and pepper.

3 Cut each chicken breast into 4 pieces. Top each with a sage leaf, then wrap as tightly as possible with a piece of pancetta.

4 Heat the olive oil in a large frying pan and brown the chicken pieces on each side. Lower the heat and continue to cook the chicken, turning, for 10 minutes, or until cooked through.

5 Serve the chicken with the greens and the roasted tomatoes, drizzled with the dressing.

PREPARE AHEAD The chicken can be covered with plastic wrap and refrigerated up to 1 day ahead.

6 servings

**prep 20 mins
• cook 1 hr
15 mins**

Guinea hen with spiced lentils

Guinea hen has a somewhat more assertive flavor than chicken, and it makes a good partner for spicy, earthy lentils.

INGREDIENTS

3lb (1.35kg) guinea hen
2 carrots, cut into chunks
2 celery stalks, halved
2 shallots, halved
1 bay leaf
10 whole black peppercorns
2 tbsp olive oil
5oz (140g) pancetta, finely diced
1 garlic clove, crushed
1 small fresh hot red chili,
    seeded and minced
1½ cups French green (Puy) lentils,
    rinsed and well drained
¼ cup chopped parsley
salt and freshly ground black pepper

METHOD

1 Put the guinea hen in a pan with the carrots, celery, shallots, bay leaf, and peppercorns. Cover with cold water, bring to the boil, then simmer for 45 minutes, covered.

2 Lift the guinea hen on to a plate; keep warm. Strain the poaching liquid back into the pan and boil for 10 minutes, or until reduced.

3 Meanwhile, heat the oil in a pan and cook the pancetta, stirring often, for about 6 minutes, or until golden. Add the garlic and chili, and cook gently for about 2 minutes, stirring often. Remove from the heat and add the lentils.

4 Pour 1¾ cups of the reduced stock into the lentils. Bring to a boil, then simmer, uncovered, for 30 minutes, until tender, adding stock as needed. Add the chopped parsley and season with salt and pepper. Meanwhile, remove the skin from the guinea hen and cut into pieces.

5 Serve the lentils, topped with pieces of guinea hen. Spoon over the stock, if desired.

4 servings

prep 20 mins
• cook 1 hr
15 mins

Lemon honey chicken breasts with mustard mayonnaise

This simple but tasty dish can be broiled or grilled.

INGREDIENTS

3 tbsp fresh lemon juice
3 tbsp balsamic vinegar
3 tbsp soy sauce
3 tbsp olive oil
2 tbsp honey
2 garlic cloves, minced
2 fresh hot red or green chilies,
   seeded and minced
6 skinless and boneless chicken breasts,
   about 6oz (175g) each

For the mustard mayonnaise

2 large egg yolks
2 tbsp sherry vinegar
1 tbsp lemon juice
1½ tsp Dijon mustard
¾ cup plus 2 tbsp vegetable oil
12 basil leaves
salt and freshly ground black pepper

METHOD

1 Mix the lemon juice, vinegar, soy sauce, oil, honey, garlic, and chilies in a zippered plastic bag. Season with the pepper. Score a shallow criss-cross pattern on the skinned side of each chicken breast, and add to the marinade. Refrigerate for at least 2 hours.

2 To make the mayonnaise, combine the egg yolks, vinegar, lemon juice, and mustard in a food processor. With the motor running, slowly add the oil in a steady stream until the mayonnaise is smooth and creamy. Add basil and pulse until chopped. Season with salt and pepper. Transfer to a bowl, cover and refrigerate for at least 1 hour.

3 Remove the chicken from the marinade. Preheat a broiler or build a fire in an outdoor grill. Add the chicken and cook about 12 minutes, until the chicken shows no sign of pink inside. Slice the chicken breasts and serve with the mayonnaise.

PREPARE AHEAD The marinating chicken and the mayonnaise can be refrigerated for up to 1 day.

6 servings

prep 25 mins,
plus marinating
• cook 15–20
mins

140

Spicy orange duck

The traditional flavor combination of rich duck and tangy orange is given a modern twist in this recipe.

INGREDIENTS

6 boneless duck breast halves, about 7oz (200g) each
salt and freshly ground black pepper
2 tbsp honey
2 scallions, white and green parts, cut into 2in (5cm) strips

For the sauce

4 large oranges
$\frac{1}{2}$ cup sugar
$\frac{1}{4}$ cup hearty red wine
$\frac{1}{2}$ inch (1cm) piece of fresh ginger, peeled and shredded
1 tbsp sweet chili dipping sauce
1 tbsp Thai fish sauce
1 tbsp rice vinegar
2 whole star anise
3in (7.5cm) cinnamon stick
1 small fresh hot red chili, seeded and finely sliced into thin rounds

METHOD

1 Preheat the oven to 425°F (220°C). To make the sauce, peel the zest from 1 orange using a vegetable peeler. Cut the zest into short thin strips. Juice the oranges to make $1\frac{1}{2}$ cups of juice. Combine the orange zest and juice with the rest of the sauce ingredients in a medium saucepan and bring to a boil, stirring. Simmer, stirring occasionally, for 12 minutes, or until lightly syrupy.

2 Trim the duck breasts of excess fat and lightly score the skin with a sharp knife. Season with salt and pepper and brush the skin with honey. Heat a large nonstick frying pan over medium-high heat. Add the duck breasts, skin side down, and cook until the skin is golden brown, about 4 minutes. Turn and cook until the flesh side is lightly browned, about 2 minutes more. Transfer the frying pan with the breast to the oven and bake for 6 minutes until the meat is still pink in the center when pierced with a sharp knife. Transfer to a carving board and let stand for 5 minutes.

3 Slice the duck and arrange the slices on dinner plates. Spoon the sauce over the duck then scatter the scallion strips on top. Serve at once.

GOOD WITH Mashed sweet potatoes and crisp-tender green beans tossed with sesame seeds.

6 servings

prep 15–20 mins
• cook 25–30 mins

Grilled poussins

Tiny poussin (baby chicken) weighs barely one pound.

INGREDIENTS
4 poussins, about 1lb (450g) each
salt and freshly ground black pepper
4 tbsp butter
2 tbsp fresh lemon juice
2 tbsp Worcestershire sauce
1 tsp dried tarragon, crumbled
1 tsp dried thyme, crumbled

METHOD
1 Position the rack about 6in (15cm) from the source of heat and preheat the broiler. Cut each poussin in half lengthwise. Season with salt and pepper. Place the poussins, skin side down, on an oiled broiler pan. Broil 20 minutes, or until lightly browned.

2 Meanwhile, in a small saucepan, melt the butter, and stir in the lemon juice, Worcestershire sauce, tarragon, and thyme. Brush the poussins with some of the butter mixture. Turn them skin side up, and brush again. Broil about 12 minutes more, basting occasionally with the butter mixture, or until golden brown and the juices run clear when pierced with a sharp knife.

GOOD WITH Mediterranean roasted vegetables, such as eggplant and zucchini.

4 servings

**prep 5 mins
• cook 30–35
mins**

Duck breasts with cherries

Many supermarkets now carry Pekin duck breasts, which are smaller than the Moulard variety.

INGREDIENTS

4 boneless duck breasts, about 7oz (200g) each
1/2 tsp salt, plus more to taste
1/2 tsp lightly crushed black peppercorns,
    plus more to taste

For the sauce

1 tbsp butter
1 shallot, finely chopped
1/3 cup ruby port
1 tbsp maple syrup
1 whole star anise
1 sprig of rosemary
1/2 cup chicken stock
2 cups pitted fresh bing cherries
salt and freshly ground black pepper

METHOD

1 Score the skin of each duck breast with a sharp knife. Season with the salt and crushed pepper.

2 Place the duck breasts, skin-side down, in a large frying pan. Cook over medium-high heat for about 8 minutes. Turn and brown the other sides, about 3 minutes for medium-rare. Transfer to a carving board and let stand for 5 minutes.

3 To make the sauce, melt the butter in a saucepan over medium heat. Add the shallot and cook, stirring often, about 2 minutes, until softened.

4 Stir in the port, maple syrup, star anise, and rosemary, and boil for 30 seconds. Add the stock and boil for about 3 minutes, or until slightly reduced. Add the cherries, and cook for 2 minutes more, until heated. Season with salt and pepper. Slice each breast on the diagaonal into thick slices and transfer each to a plate. Top with the sauce and serve hot.

PREPARE AHEAD The sauce can be made and refrigerated up to 2 days in advance.

4 servings

prep 15 mins
• cook 20 mins

Crispy roast duck

This Asian method of cooking duck makes the most of its sweet, succulent flesh.

INGREDIENTS
1 duck, about 1½lb (1.6kg)
3 tbsp oyster sauce
1 tsp Chinese five-spice powder
1 tsp salt

For the glaze
3 tbsp honey
2 tbsp Chinese rice wine or dry sherry
1 tbsp dark soy sauce

METHOD
1 Rinse the duck inside and out with cold running water. Pat dry with paper towels. Mix together the oyster sauce, five-spice powder, and salt and spread it inside the duck.

2 Bring a large kettle of water to a boil. Tie some kitchen twine under the wings so the duck can be hung up. Place the duck in a colander in the sink. Pour boiling water over the duck—the skin will tighten. Pat the duck with paper towels. Repeat the pouring and drying process five more times.

3 To make the glaze, bring the honey, rice wine, soy sauce, and ²/₃ cup water to a boil over high heat. Reduce the heat to medium-low and simmer briskly about 12 minutes, or until sticky. Let cool slightly. Brush the glaze all over the duck.

4 Hang the duck over a roasting pan in a cool place. Train an electric fan on the duck. Let stand for about 4 hours, or until the skin is dry.

5 Preheat the oven to 450°F (230°C). Place the duck on a rack in a roasting pan, breast side up. Pour 2 cups water into the pan. Roast for 20 minutes. Reduce the oven temperature to 350°F (180°C) and roast for 1 hour 15 minutes, or until the duck skin is shiny, crisp, and golden brown.

6 Let stand for 10 minutes. Using a large, sharp knife, cut into quarters. Arrange the duck on a serving platter and serve hot.

GOOD WITH Chinese pancakes, shredded spring onions, thin batons of cucumber, and hoisin sauce.

PREPARE AHEAD The duck must be air-dried for several hours before roasting.

2–4 servings

prep 1 hr 15 mins,
plus drying and
resting • cook
1 hr 35 mins

meat hook or
kitchen twine

Chicken in a pot

A simple meal wonderfully flavored with hard apple cider and root vegetables.

INGREDIENTS

1 chicken, about 3¾lb (1.7kg), trussed
2 tbsp vegetable oil
1 tbsp all-purpose flour
2 cups hard apple cider
1 cup chicken stock
1 bouquet garni (1 celery stalk,
    4 thyme sprigs, 4 parsley sprigs tied)
salt and freshly ground black pepper
12oz (350g) baby carrots, peeled
12oz (350g) baby new potatoes,
    scrubbed, but unpeeled
2 leeks, thickly sliced
¼ cup chopped fresh parsley

METHOD

1 Preheat the oven to 325°F (160°C). Using kitchen twine, tie the chicken drumsticks together. Tie twine across the breast to secure the wings down. Heat the oil in the casserole over medium heat. Add the chicken and brown on all sides. Transfer to a plate. Sprinkle flour into the casserole and stir for 2 minutes over low heat until barely browned. Stir in the cider and stock, and bring to a boil.

2 Return the chicken to the casserole, breast-side up. Add the bouquet garni and salt and pepper to taste. Cover and bake for 1¼ hours. Add the carrots, potatoes, and leeks. Return to the oven and bake for about 40 minutes more, or until the juices run clear when pierced.

3 Transfer the chicken to a carving board. Let stand for 10 minutes. Discard the bouquet garni. Carve the chicken, return to the pot, and sprinkle with parsley. Serve hot.

GOOD WITH Creamy mashed potatoes and green beans or a green leafy vegetable. Leftovers can be tossed with frisée, grated carrot, and vinaigrette dressing to make a salad.

4 servings

prep 10 mins
• cook 1¾ hrs

large flame-proof casserole

freeze after step 3, once cooled completely, for up to 3 months; thaw at room temperature, then reheat

Roast chicken

Impressive, classic, and simple to cook, the perfect roast chicken is all about timing and turning.

INGREDIENTS
1 oven-ready chicken, about 2.2kg (5lb)
30g (1oz) butter or 2 tbsp olive oil
salt and freshly ground black pepper
300g (10oz) stuffing of your choice (optional)

METHOD
1 Preheat the oven to 200°C (400°F/Gas 6). Weigh the chicken and calculate the cooking time allowing 20 minutes per 450g (1lb), plus 20 minutes. Put the bird on a clean cutting board and remove the wishbone (see page 20).

2 Rub the bird with the butter, then season well with salt and pepper inside and out, and place in a roasting tin. (If you are stuffing your bird, it's worth taking the trouble to do so between the breast and the skin (see page 21). This will protect and flavour the breast as it cooks.)

3 Place the bird in the middle shelf of the oven and roast for the calculated time. Baste the chicken regularly and turn it breast-side down for about a third of the cooking time to ensure the meat cooks evenly.

4 To check whether the chicken is cooked, pierce the thickest part of the leg with a metal skewer or thin knife to see if the juices run clear. If the juices are still pink, cook for a further 15 minutes, then check again. Leave the bird to rest for 15 minutes, then carve and serve.

GOOD WITH Bread sauce, gravy, and a selection of steamed vegetables.

serves 6

prep 15 mins
• cook 20 mins
per 450g (1lb)
and an extra 20
mins, plus 15
mins resting

low GI

French roast chicken

The method of herb butter slipped under the chicken's skin makes for a very tasty chicken.

INGREDIENTS

8 tbsp butter, softened
¼ cup chopped herbs, such as tarragon,
   parsley, and/or chives, plus sprigs to garnish
2 garlic cloves, finely chopped
1 chicken, about 4lb (1.8kg)
1 lemon
salt and freshly ground black pepper
2 cups chicken stock
½ cup dry white wine, as needed

METHOD

1 Preheat the oven to 375°F (190°C). Mash the butter, herbs, and garlic together and beat. Ease your fingers between the breast skin and chicken flesh, being careful not to tear the skin. Tuck the butter under the skin. Pierce the lemon all over with a fork and place inside the body cavity. Truss with kitchen twine, if desired. Season with salt and pepper.

2 Put the chicken on a rack in the roasting pan. Pour 1½ cups of the stock and the wine over the chicken. Roast for about 1½ hours, or until an instant-read thermometer inserted in the thickest part of the thigh, not touching a bone, reads 170°F (77°C). If the liquid evaporates from the bottom of the pan, add a little more wine.

3 Transfer the chicken to a platter. Cover with aluminum foil and let stand for 10 minutes. Spoon off the fat from the pan. Add the remaining ½ cup stock and bring to a boil over high heat. Boil, stirring often, about 3 minutes, until slightly reduced. Garnish the chicken with the herb sprigs and serve hot, with the pan juices.

PREPARE AHEAD The herb butter can be refrigerated up to 1 day ahead; bring to room temperature before using.

4 servings

**prep 15 mins
• cook 1 hr
30 mins**

Chicken with thyme and lemon

The combination of lemon, thyme, and a light, buttery glaze make this chicken a special dinner dish.

INGREDIENTS

1 chicken, about 4lb (1.8kg),
   cut into 8 pieces (see page 12)
salt and freshly ground black pepper
1 lemon
1 tbsp butter, softened
1 tbsp olive oil
2 tsp chopped thyme
2 garlic cloves, minced
1/2 cup dry white wine

METHOD

1 Preheat the oven to 400°F (200°C). Spread the chicken in a single layer in a roasting pan. Season with salt and pepper.

2 Grate the lemon zest into a bowl. Add the butter, oil, thyme, and garlic, and combine.

3 Dot the lemon and thyme mixture evenly over the chicken. Cut the reserved lemon into chunks and tuck around the chicken. Pour the wine over the chicken.

4 Roast the chicken for 50–60 minutes. Turn and baste the chicken occasionally, until the chicken is golden brown and the juices run clear when the meat is pierced with a knife. Add a little more wine if the juices cook away. Serve hot.

GOOD WITH A mixed salad and oven-baked potato wedges.

4 servings

prep 15 mins,
plus standing
• cook 1 hr

low fat

Guinea hen breasts with mustard sauce

Guinea hen is less gamey in flavor than grouse.

INGREDIENTS

1 tbsp vegetable oil
4 skinless and boneless guinea hen breasts
salt and freshly ground black pepper

For the mustard sauce

$\frac{1}{2}$ cup dry vermouth or sherry
$\frac{2}{3}$ cup chicken stock
1 cup heavy cream
2 tsp whole grain mustard
1 tbsp chopped chives

METHOD

1 To make the sauce, reduce the vermouth by half in a saucepan over high heat. Add the stock, boil, and reduce by half again. Add the cream and cook until thick. Set aside.

2 Meanwhile, preheat the oven to 475°F (240°C). Heat the oil in an ovenproof frying pan over high heat. Add the breasts skin-side down and cook about 4 minutes. Flip and season with salt and pepper. Transfer to the oven and roast about 10 minutes, until the juices run clear when pierced with a fork. Transfer to a platter.

3 Pour the fat from the skillet and return to medium heat. Add the sauce and stir to loosen the browned bits in the pan. Whisk in the mustard and chives. Slice the breasts and spoon the sauce on top. Serve hot.

GOOD WITH Buttered new potatoes and sautéed onions.

4 servings

prep 40 mins
• cook 25 mins

Roast goose

Goose meat is rich in flavor, making it a perfect choice for a festive dinner party or special holiday meal.

INGREDIENTS
1 goose, thawed, 11$\frac{1}{4}$lb (5kg)
salt and freshly ground black pepper
2 small onions, cut in half
$\frac{2}{3}$ cup hearty red wine

METHOD
1 Preheat the oven to 350°F (180°C). Prick the skin all over with a meat fork, rub with salt, and sprinkle with pepper. Tuck 2 onion halves in the neck cavity and the 2 halves in the body cavity.

2 Place the goose, breast side up, on a rack in a roasting pan. Cover the pan tightly with aluminum foil. Roast for about 3 hours, occasionally basting the goose with the fat in the pan, until the goose is a rich amber brown color and a meat thermometer, inserted in the thickest part of the thigh, reads 180°F (85°C). Remove the foil during the last 40 minutes.

3 Transfer the goose to a serving platter and tent with foil. Let stand 20 minutes before carving. Carefully pour off the pan juices and fat into a heatproof bowl. Skim off the fat and reserve the pan juices. (Save the fat for another use, if you wish.)

4 Heat the pan over high heat, add the red wine, and scrape up the browned bits in the pan with a wooden spoon. Pour in the skimmed juices. Boil about 2 minutes, until slightly reduced.

5 Carve the goose and serve with the wine sauce.

GOOD WITH A selection of roast vegetables, such as potatoes, carrots, and parsnips.

6 servings

prep 20 mins
• cook 3 hrs

freeze, cooked,
for up to
3 months

Roast turkey with spiked gravy

Everyone needs a solid recipe for the holiday turkey, and this one fits the bill.

INGREDIENTS

14lb (6.3kg) turkey
cornbread stuffing
8 tbsp butter, softened
salt and freshly ground black pepper
6 tbsp all-purpose flour
3 cups turkey or chicken stock, as needed
$^1\!/_4$ cup bourbon (optional)

METHOD

1 Preheat the oven to 325°F (165°C). Remove the neck, giblets, and fat from the tail area and save for another use. Stuff the neck cavity loosely with stuffing, and pin the neck skin to the back with a skewer. Loosely fill the body cavity with the stuffing and cover the exposed stuffing with foil. Using kitchen twine, tie the drumsticks together and secure the wings to the body.

2 Place the turkey on a rack in a roasting pan. Rub with the butter and season with salt and pepper. Loosely cover the breast area with foil. Add 2 cups water to the pan.

3 Roast, basting every hour or so (lifting the foil to do so), estimating about 15 minutes per pound, for about 3$^1\!/_2$ hours, until an instant-read thermometer inserted in the thickest part of the thigh, not allowing it to touch a bone, reads 175°F (79°C). During the last hour of cooking, remove the foil. Transfer the turkey to a platter. Let stand for 30 minutes.

4 Meanwhile, make the gravy. Pour the pan drippings into a glass bowl. Skim off and measure 6 tbsp fat; discard remaining fat. Add enough stock to degreased drippings to make 1 quart (1 liter).

5 Place the pan over medium heat. Add the fat, whisk in the flour, and let cook 1 minute. Whisk in the stock mixture and bourbon, if using, scraping up the browned bits, and bring to a boil. Simmer over low heat, whisking often, until thickened, about 10 minutes. Season with salt and pepper and pour into a sauceboat.

6 Carve the turkey and serve with the gravy.

GOOD WITH The traditional accompaniments of sweet potatoes, cranberry sauce, mashed potatoes, and green beans or Brussels sprouts.

12 servings

prep 30 mins
• cook 3½ hrs

low fat

freeze the
cooked turkey
and stuffing
for up to
3 months

LEFTOVERS

Chicken stock

Endlessly versatile, homemade chicken stock is well worth the effort.

INGREDIENTS

3lb (1.3kg) chicken wings,
   chopped at the joints
2 celery stalks, roughly chopped
2 onions, quartered
8 sprigs parsley
4 sprigs thyme
1 bay leaf
1 tsp salt
10 whole black peppercorns,
   lightly crushed

METHOD

1 Combine the chicken, celery, and onion in a large saucepan with 2 qts (2 liters) cold water. Bring just to a boil over high heat. Using a large spoon, skim off any foam that rises to the surface. Reduce the heat to low and add the parsley, thyme, bay leaf, salt, and peppercorns. Partially cover the saucepan. Simmer for at least 1 and up to 3 hours.

2 Strain the stock into a large bowl. Let stand 10 minutes, then skim the fat from the surface. Use immediately, or cool completely and refrigerate or freeze.

PREPARE AHEAD The stock can be cooled, covered, and refrigerated for up to 2 days. Scrape any residual fat from the surface.

**makes about
2 qts (2 liters)**

**prep 10 mins
• cook 1 hr**

**freeze for up to
6 months**

Club sandwich

Here is a hearty sandwich of chicken, bacon, tomatoes, and lettuce, layered between slices of toasted bread, guaranteed to satisfy those hunger pangs.

INGREDIENTS

1 tsp dried Italian herbs
2 tbsp olive oil
1 small garlic clove, crushed
salt and freshly ground black pepper
3 boneless and skinless chicken breasts
16 slices bacon
12 slices white sandwich bread
⅓ cup mayonnaise
1 tsp whole grain mustard
4 ripe tomatoes, sliced
½ head romaine lettuce, shredded
8 small sour pickles (cornichons)

METHOD

1 Mix together the herbs, 1 tbsp olive oil, and garlic in a bowl and season with salt and pepper. Add the chicken breasts, toss to coat, and set aside for 30 to 90 minutes.

2 Meanwhile, heat the remaining oil in a large frying pan over medium heat. In batches, cook the bacon for about 5 minutes, until crisp and golden. Using a slotted spatula, transfer to paper towels, leaving the fat in the pan.

3 Add the chicken breasts to the pan and cook for about 5 minutes on each side until the flesh feels firm when pressed in the center. Transfer to a plate.

4 Meanwhile, toast the bread. Arrange the slices on a large cutting board. Trim the crusts if desired. Cut the bacon slices in half.

5 In a small bowl, mix together the mayonnaise and mustard. Spread the toast with the mayonnaise mixture. Slice the chicken breasts against the grain. Arrange half of the chicken on four of the toasted bread slices. Top the chicken with half of the bacon, tomato slices, and lettuce. Top each with a slice of toast. Repeat with the remaining chicken, bacon, tomatoes, and lettuce, then top with the remaining 4 slices of toast, mayonnaise-side down.

6 Cut each sandwich in half, diagonally. Push a cocktail toothpick through the center of each triangle to hold it together, and top each with a pickle.

GOOD WITH Sweet or dill gherkins and other pickles on the side.

PREPARE AHEAD The recipe can be made through step 5 up to 2 hours in advance.

4 servings

prep 15 mins,
plus marinating
• cook 15 mins

Meaty spring rolls

These get their name because they were served to commemorate the first day of Spring in the Chinese calendar.

INGREDIENTS

8oz (225g) cooked ham, chopped,
  or other meats such as pork or beef
1 cup bean sprouts
1/2 red bell pepper, cored, seeded, and finely chopped
4oz (115g) shiitake mushrooms, stemmed and chopped
4 scallions, green and white parts, thinly sliced
3/4in (2cm) piece of fresh ginger, peeled and grated
1 tbsp rice wine or cider vinegar
1 tbsp soy sauce
2 tbsp vegetable oil, plus more for deep-frying
1 cup chopped cooked chicken
6 napa cabbage leaves, tough stalks cut away
1 tbsp cornstarch, plus more for the baking sheet
12 spring roll wrappers
sweet chili dipping sauce, to serve

METHOD

1 In a bowl, mix together the ham, bean sprouts, red pepper, mushrooms, scallions, ginger, vinegar, and soy sauce.

2 Heat 2 tbsp oil in a frying pan over medium-high heat. Add the shrimp mixture and stir-fry for 3 minutes. Set aside to cool, then stir in the chicken.

3 In a bowl, mix the cornstarch with 4 tbsp cold water.

4 Dust a baking sheet with cornstarch. Lay a wrapper on a work surface. Top with half a cabbage leaf and 1 tbsp of the ham mixture. Brush the edges with the dissolved cornstarch and roll up around the filling, tucking in the sides and pressing together to seal. Place on the baking sheet. Repeat with the remaining wrappers and filling.

5 Line another baking sheet with paper towels. Preheat the oven to 200°F (100°C). Pour 1/4in (5mm) oil into a large frying pan. In batches, add the rolls and fry, turning occasionally, about 4 minutes, or until golden. Transfer to paper towels to drain. Keep warm in the oven while frying the remaining rolls. Serve hot, with the chili sauce for dipping.

PREPARE AHEAD Make the filling up to 3 hours in advance and fill the rolls just before frying.

12 rolls

prep 25 mins
• cook 15 mins

Calzone

These folded pizzas have a tasty chicken, pancetta, and vegetable filling.

INGREDIENTS

$3^2/_3$ cups bread flour

two $^1/_4$ oz (7g) envelopes instant yeast

$^1/_2$ tsp salt

$1^1/_2$ cups tepid water

2 tbsp olive oil, plus more for the bowl

For the filling

3 tbsp olive oil, plus more for the baking sheets

6 slices pancetta, chopped

1 boneless skinless chicken breast, cut into small pieces

1 green bell pepper, seeded and chopped

$^1/_4$ cup sun-dried tomato paste

7oz (200g) mozzarella cheese, sliced

$^1/_4$ cup chopped parsley

freshly ground black pepper

1 large beaten egg, to seal

METHOD

1 Combine the flour, yeast, and salt in a large bowl. Make a well in the center, add the water and oil, and stir to make a soft dough. Knead on a lightly floured work surface about 10 minutes, until smooth and elastic.

2 Roll the dough into a ball. Place in a lightly oiled bowl and turn to coat the dough. Cover tightly with plastic wrap. Let stand in a warm place until doubled in size.

3 Preheat the oven to 400°F (200°C). Divide the dough into four equal portions. Roll out each on a lightly floured work surface into a 9in (23cm) round.

4 Heat 1 tbsp of the oil in a frying pan over medium-high heat. Add the pancetta, chicken, and green pepper and cook until the chicken is opaque throughout, about 5 minutes. Transfer to a bowl and let cool.

5 Spread the tomato paste over the lower half of each dough round, leaving a $^1/_2$in (13mm) border. Divide the filling evenly over the paste, then top with equal amounts of the mozzarella and parsley. Season generously with the pepper.

6 Brush the exposed edges of the dough with the beaten egg. Fold over to enclose the filling, pressing the edges together firmly with your fingers or a fork to seal.

7 Brush with the remaining olive oil. Bake for 20–25 minutes or until the edges are crisp and golden brown. Serve hot.

GOOD WITH A green salad.

PREPARE AHEAD The dough can be refrigerated in an airtight container for up to 1 day. Let stand in a warm place about $2^1/_2$ hours, untill doubled, and knead briefly before using.

4 calzones

prep 20 mins, plus cooling • cook 25–30 mins

Cock-a-leekie soup

In days past, this soup involved the slow simmering of a whole chicken, but today it is prepared with less time and effort.

INGREDIENTS
1lb (450g) chicken breasts and/or thighs, skinned
1 quart (1 liter) chicken stock
2 bay leaves
⅓ cup long-grain rice
2 leeks, white and pale green parts only,
   cleaned and thinly sliced
2 carrots, shredded
pinch of ground cloves
salt and freshly ground pepper
1 tbsp chopped parsley

METHOD
1 Combine the chicken, stock, and bay leaves in a large saucepan and bring to a boil over high heat, skimming off any foam. Reduce the heat to medium-low and cover. Simmer, skimming occasionally, for 30 minutes.

2 Add the rice, leeks, carrots, and cloves, and season with salt and pepper. Return to a boil over high heat, then reduce the heat to medium-low, and cover again. Simmer about 30 minutes more, until the chicken shows no sign of pink at the bone.

3 Discard the bay leaves. Transfer the chicken to a carving board, cool, remove the meat from the bones, chop it into bite-sized pieces, and return it to the soup.

4 Ladle the soup into bowls and sprinkle with parsley. Serve hot.

GOOD WITH Warm crusty bread.

4 servings

prep 10 mins
• cook 1½ hrs

low fat

freeze for up to
3 months

177

Mexican chicken noodle soup

This spicy Mexican soup has thin *fideo* noodles—similar to angel hair pasta—and makes a substantial meal.

INGREDIENTS

2 large ripe tomatoes, skinned and seeded
1 small onion, roughly chopped
2 canned chipotle chilies en adobo
   or 2 dried chipotle chilies, soaked
2 garlic cloves
3 tbsp vegetable oil
2 boneless and skinless chicken breasts,
   cut into bite-sized pieces
3³/₄ cups chicken stock
8oz (225g) Mexican *fideos* or angel hair pasta

To serve

¹/₄ cup sour cream
1 avocado, peeled, pitted, and cubed

METHOD

1 Purée the tomatoes, onion, chilies, and garlic in a food processor.

2 Heat 2 tbsp of the oil in a large saucepan over medium-high heat. Add the chicken and stir-fry for 2–3 minutes, or until just cooked. Using a slotted spoon, transfer to a plate.

3 Add the remaining 1 tbsp oil to the pan and heat. Reduce the heat to medium-low. Add the noodles and cook, turning once, about 2 minutes, until golden.

4 Add the tomato purée and stir until the noodles are coated. Stir in the stock and return the chicken to the saucepan. Return the heat to high and cook until the noodles are tender.

5 Ladle the soup into bowls and top each serving with a dollop of sour cream and some avocado cubes. Serve hot.

PREPARE AHEAD The soup can be refrigerated for up to 3 days.

4 servings

prep 20 mins • cook 15 mins

if using dried chilies, soak for 30 mins first

low fat

Warm chicken salad

Quick to cook and easy to assemble, this warm salad is hearty, but refreshing at the same time.

INGREDIENTS

4 tbsp extra virgin olive oil
4 skinless, boneless chicken breasts, about 5½oz (150g) each,
    cut into ½in (1cm) wide strips
⅓ cup drained and thinly sliced sun-dried tomatoes in olive oil
1 garlic clove, finely chopped
salt and freshly ground black pepper
1 small head radicchio, torn into small pieces
9oz (250g) asparagus spears, trimmed and each cut into 3 pieces
2 tbsp raspberry vinegar
½ tsp sugar

METHOD

1 Heat 2 tbsp of the oil in a large non-stick frying pan over medium-high heat. Add the chicken, sun-dried tomatoes, and garlic. Season with salt and pepper. Cook, stirring often, for 5 minutes, or until the chicken is opaque when pierced with the tip of a knife.

2 Meanwhile, put the radicchio in a large serving bowl. Using a slotted spoon, add the chicken mixture to the radicchio.

3 Add the asparagus pieces to the fat remaining in the pan and stir-fry for 1–2 minutes, or until they are crisp-tender. Transfer to the bowl with the chicken.

4 Whisk together the remaining 2 tbsp oil, the vinegar, and sugar in a bowl, then pour into the pan, and stir over high heat until hot. Pour the vinaigrette over the salad, and toss quickly to combine. Serve immediately.

GOOD WITH Thick slices of crusty French bread.

4 servings

**prep 10 mins
• cook 8 mins**

Chicken and noodle stir-fry

A colorful Chinese favorite, this dish is packed with contrasting flavors and textures.

INGREDIENTS

12oz (350g) fresh Asian egg noodles or fresh fettucine
3 tbsp vegetable oil
2 skinless boneless chicken breasts,
    cut into bite-sized pieces
1/2 red, green, and yellow or orange pepper,
    seeded and sliced
4oz (115g) shiitake mushrooms, quartered
1 tbsp peeled and shredded fresh ginger
1/2 cup chicken stock
2 tbsp ketchup
2 tbsp soy sauce
1 tsp cornstarch
few drops of Asian sesame oil
2 tbsp sesame seeds, for garnish

METHOD

1 Bring a saucepan of lightly salted water to a boil. Cook the noodles about 2 minutes, until barely tender. Drain and rinse under cold running water. Toss with 1 tbsp oil.

2 Heat 1 tbsp of the oil in the wok over high heat. Add the chicken and stir-fry for 3 minutes. Remove and set aside. Add the peppers, mushrooms, and ginger to the wok and stir-fry for another 3 minutes.

3 Mix together the chicken stock, ketchup, soy sauce, and cornstarch. Return the chicken to the wok, add the noodles, and pour in the stock mixture. Stir-fry for 3 minutes, until the chicken is cooked through. Just before serving, drizzle with the sesame oil and sprinkle with the sesame seeds.

4 servings

prep 20 mins
• cook 10 mins

wok

Chicken croquettes

These savory nuggets, crunchy outside and meltingly soft inside, are a fine way to use leftover chicken. Here is a Spanish version.

INGREDIENTS

5 tbsp butter
⅓ cup all-purpose flour
1¾ cups whole milk
1 cup finely chopped cooked chicken
1 tsp tomato paste
salt and freshly ground black pepper
¾ cup dried bread crumbs
3 large eggs
vegetable oil, for deep-frying

METHOD

1 Melt the butter in a medium saucepan over medium-low heat. Whisk in the flour. Let bubble without browning for 2 minutes. Whisk in the milk and increase the heat to medium. Bring to a boil, whisking often. Reduce the heat to low and cook, whisking often, until the sauce is very thick, about 5 minutes.

2 Stir in the chicken and tomato paste and season with salt and pepper. Transfer the mixture to a bowl. Press a piece of plastic wrap directly on the surface and pierce a few holes in the wrap. Let stand about 2 hours, until completely cooled.

3 Line a baking sheet with wax paper. Spread the bread crumbs in a shallow dish. Beat the eggs in another shallow dish. Use two soup spoons to form 12 thick ovals about 1½–2in (3–4cm) long. Roll in the bread crumbs, coat with the eggs, roll again in the bread crumbs, and place on the baking sheet.

4 Preheat the oven to 200°F (100°C). Line another baking sheet with paper towels. Add enough oil to a large, heavy frying pan to come halfway up the sides and heat until the oil is 350°F (170°C). In two batches, add the croquettes and deep-fry, turning frequently, about 3 minutes, or until deep golden brown. Transfer to the paper towels, and keep warm in the oven.

5 Serve the croquettes on a heated serving platter.

GOOD WITH Garlic mayonnaise or *Salsa Rosa*, made from 2 parts mayonnaise to 1 part tomato ketchup. The croquettes can also be served cold, making them excellent picnic food.

PREPARE AHEAD The béchamel sauce can be prepared ahead and allowed to cool. The croquettes can be made up to 24 hours in advance and fried before serving.

4 servings

**prep 30 mins
• cook 20 mins**

**freeze for up to
3 months**

Chicken chow mein

This popular one-pot Chinese dish is a colorful, tasty medley of noodles, chicken, mushrooms, and vegetables.

INGREDIENTS
12oz (350g) fresh Asian-style egg noodles or linguine
4 tbsp plus 1 tsp vegetable oil
½ cup chicken stock
¼ cup soy sauce, plus more to serve
1 tbsp rice wine or dry sherry
1 tsp cornstarch
4 scallions, white and green parts,
  cut into 1in (2.5cm) lengths
5oz (140g) shiitake mushrooms,
  stemmed and sliced
1 small red pepper, seeded and chopped
one ¾in (2cm) piece of fresh ginger,
  peeled and shredded
6 skinless and boneless chicken thighs,
  cut into bite-sized pieces
4oz (115g) green beans, cut into 1in (2.5cm) lengths

METHOD
1 Bring a large pot of lightly salted water to a boil over high heat. Add the noodles and cook according to the package instructions. Drain and rinse under cold running water. Drain and toss with 1 tsp of the oil. Mix the stock, soy sauce, and rice wine in a bowl, sprinkle in the cornstarch and stir to dissolve.

2 Heat 1 tbsp of the oil in a wok or large frying pan over high heat. Add the scallions, mushrooms, red pepper, and ginger. Stir-fry until crisp-tender, about 3 minutes. Transfer to a plate.

3 Heat 2 tbsp of the oil and heat. In two batches, add the chicken and stir-fry until the chicken is cooked through, about 5 minutes. Transfer to the vegetables.

4 Add the remaining 1 tbsp oil to the wok and heat. Add the green beans and stir-fry for 2 minutes or until crisp-tender.

5 Add the noodles and return the chicken and vegetables to the wok. Add the stock mixture and stir-fry about 2 minutes, or until the noodles are piping hot. Serve at once, with soy sauce for seasoning.

GOOD WITH Other Chinese dishes, as part of a themed meal.

4 servings

prep 15 mins
• cook 15 mins

low in
saturated fat

Chicken pasties

A complete and filling lunch fits in these pastry packets.

INGREDIENTS

For the dough
2$\frac{1}{3}$ cups all-purpose flour
12 tbsp cold butter, diced
2 large eggs

For the filling
$\frac{1}{2}$ cup cream cheese
4 scallions, thinly sliced
2 tbsp chopped parsley
salt and freshly ground black pepper
12oz (350g) boneless and skinless chicken breast,
    cut into $\frac{3}{4}$ in (2cm) dice
1 red-skinned potato, peeled and cut into $\frac{1}{2}$in (1cm) dice
1 small sweet potato, peeled and cut into $\frac{1}{2}$in (1cm) dice

METHOD

1 To make the dough, sift the flour into a bowl, then rub in the butter until the mixture resembles fine bread crumbs. Beat the eggs and 3 tbsp of cold water together. Set aside 1 tbsp of the mixture for glazing, and pour the rest over the dry ingredients, and mix to a dough. Wrap in plastic wrap and refrigerate for 20 minutes.

2 Meanwhile, mix the cream cheese, scallions, and parsley in a bowl, and season to taste with salt and pepper. Stir in the chicken, potato, and sweet potato.

3 Preheat the oven to 400°F (200°C). Divide the dough into 4 pieces. Roll out each piece on a lightly floured surface. Using a small plate as a guide, cut into an 8in (20cm) round about $\frac{1}{8}$in (3mm) thick.

4 Spoon a quarter of the filling into the center of each round. Brush the edges with water and bring together to seal, then crimp. Transfer the pasties to a baking sheet.

5 Brush with the reserved egg mixture. Make a slit in the tops and bake for 10 minutes, then reduce the heat to 350°F (180°C) and cook for 25–30 minutes, or until a thin knife comes out clean when inserted into the center.

6 Remove from the oven and serve the pasties hot or cold.

4 servings

prep 30 mins,
plus chilling
• cook 35 mins

Chicken jalousie

Although it looks impressive, this dish is quick to make with store-bought puff pastry and leftover chicken.

INGREDIENTS

2 tbsp butter
2 leeks, white and pale green part only,
    cleaned and thinly sliced
2 tsp all-purpose flour, plus more for rolling
$\frac{1}{2}$ cup chicken stock
$2\frac{1}{2}$ cups chopped boneless cooked chicken
1 tsp chopped thyme
1 tsp fresh lemon juice
salt and freshly ground black pepper
one 17.3oz (484g) box thawed frozen puff pastry
1 large egg, beaten

METHOD

1 Melt the butter in a saucepan over low heat. Add the leeks and cook for 5 minutes until tender. Sprinkle in the flour and stir. Stir in the stock and bring to a boil, stirring often. Remove from the heat and stir in the chicken, thyme, and lemon juice. Season well with salt and pepper. Cover with plastic wrap and let cool.

2 Preheat the oven to 425°F (220°C). Dampen a large baking sheet. Roll out one sheet of the puff pastry on a lightly floured surface. Trim into a 10 x 6in (30 x 15cm) rectangle. Place the pastry on the baking sheet. Roll out and trim the remaining pastry to 10 x 7in (30 x 18cm) rectangle. Lightly dust it with flour, then fold in half lengthwise. Make cuts $\frac{1}{2}$in (1cm) apart along the folded edge to within 1in (2.5cm) of the outer edge.

3 Spoon evenly over the puff pastry base, leaving a 1in (2.5cm) border. Dampen the edges of the pastry with water. Place the second piece of pastry on top and press the edges together to seal; trim off the excess. Brush with beaten egg. Bake for 25 minutes or until golden-brown and crisp. Cool briefly, then slice and serve hot.

GOOD WITH Roasted vegetables such as zucchini and eggplant.

4 servings

prep 25 mins
• cook 25 mins

Chinese rice porridge

Known in Asia as Rice Congee or *Jook*, it is eaten for breakfast in China when the weather is cold.

INGREDIENTS

6 dried shiitake mushrooms
2 tbsp vegetable oil
½in (1 cm) piece fresh ginger,
    peeled and grated
1 garlic clove, finely chopped
1 carrot, cut into julienne strips
½ tsp crushed hot red pepper
1 cup long-grain rice
3½ cups chicken stock
2 boneless and skinless chicken breasts, finely diced
2 scallions, white and green parts, chopped
2 tbsp soy sauce
freshly ground black pepper
2 tbsp chopped cilantro

METHOD

1 Put the mushrooms in a small bowl and add a cup of boiling water. Let stand about 20 minutes, until softened. Drain, reserving the soaking water. Cut the mushrooms into small pieces using kitchen scissors, discarding the stems.

2 Heat the oil in a wok over low heat. Add the carrot, ginger, garlic, and crushed peppers and cook gently for 5 minutes. Stir in the rice and pour in the stock. Measure two-thirds of the mushroom water and strain through a fine sieve into the rice mixture.

3 Reduce the heat to medium-low and simmer, stirring often, about 40 minutes. Add the chicken and cook for 10 minutes, or until the rice has broken down to a porridge-like consistency. Stir in the scallions, soy sauce, season with pepper, and sprinkle with the cilantro. Serve hot.

PREPARE AHEAD The porridge can be made up to 2 hours ahead and reheated, adding stock or water if it has become too thick.

4 servings

prep 20 mins,
plus standing
• cook 1 hr

low fat

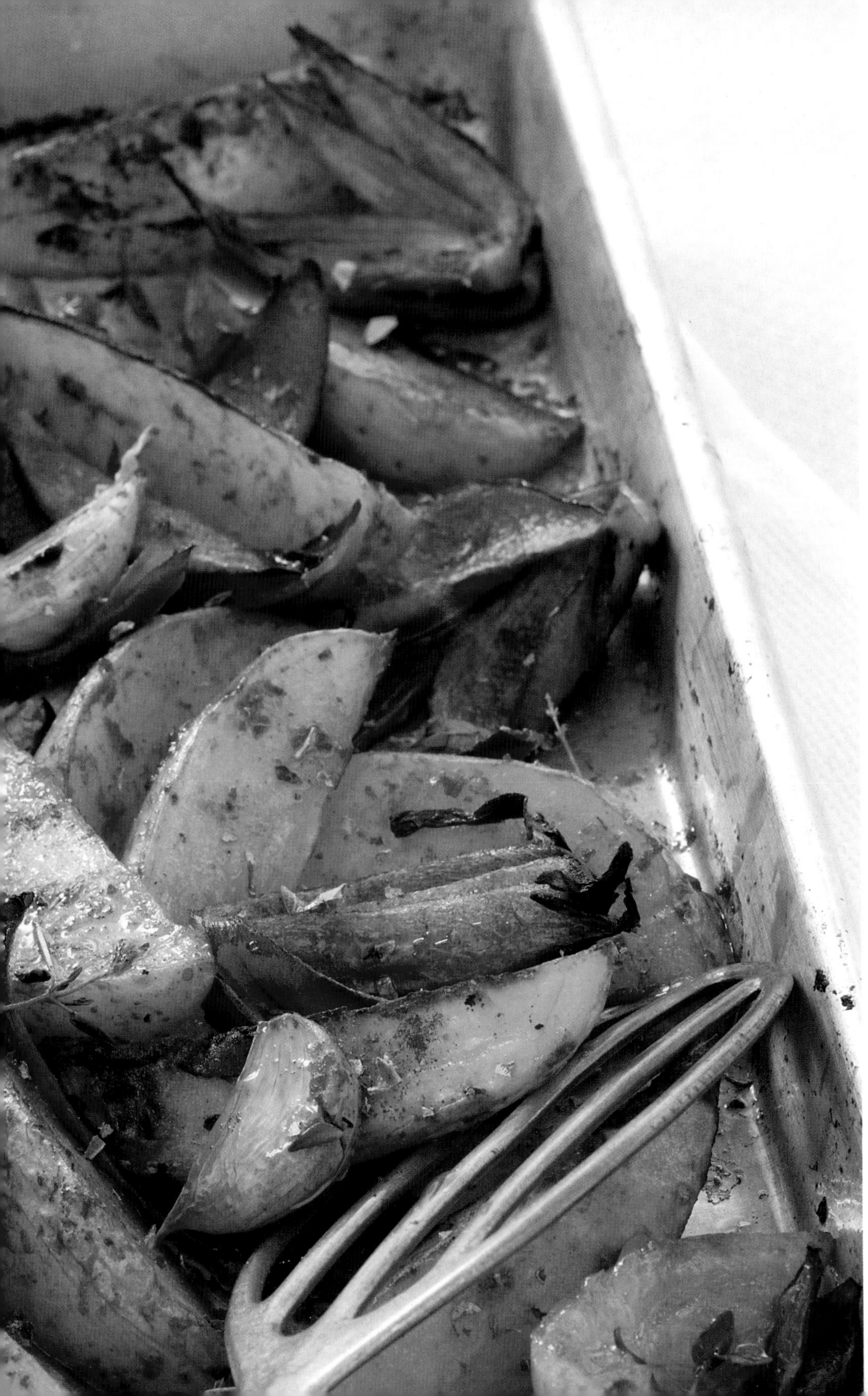

ACCOMPANIMENTS

Rice and peas

This dish is a staple throughout the Caribbean. Pigeon peas can be found in the Latin section of the market.

INGREDIENTS

15oz (420g) can pigeon peas (gandules) drained and rinsed
one 15fl oz (420ml) can coconut milk
1 large onion, finely chopped
1 green bell pepper, seeded and chopped
salt and freshly ground black pepper
¾ cup basmati or long-grain rice
cayenne pepper, for garnish

METHOD

1 Bring the peas, coconut milk, onion, and green pepper to a simmer in a saucepan over low heat and cook for 5 minutes. Season with salt and pepper.

2 Stir in the rice. Cover and simmer for 35 minutes, or until the rice is tender, stirring occasionally. Sprinkle with cayenne pepper and serve hot.

PREPARE AHEAD The dish can be prepared 1 day in advance, cooled, covered with foil, and refrigerated. Bake, covered, in a 350°F (180°C) oven until heated through.

4 servings

prep 10 mins
• cook 45 mins

Cajun-spiced potato wedges

This peppery dish was developed by the French settlers of Louisiana.

INGREDIENTS
4 potatoes, unpeeled
3 red onions, cut into 8 wedges
1 lemon, cut into 6 wedges
12 garlic cloves, unpeeled
4 bay leaves
$\frac{1}{3}$ cup olive oil
3 tbsp fresh lemon juice
1 tbsp tomato paste
1 tsp sweet paprika
1 tsp dried oregano
1 tsp dried thyme
$\frac{1}{2}$ tsp cayenne pepper
$\frac{1}{2}$ tsp ground cumin
salt and freshly ground black pepper

METHOD
1 Preheat the oven to 400°F (200°C). Cut the potatoes into thick wedges. Parcook in a large pan of salted boiling water for 3 minutes. Drain well. Combine the potatoes, onions, lemon, garlic, and bay leaves in a large roasting pan.

2 Whisk together the oil, lemon juice, tomato paste, paprika, oregano, thyme, cayenne, and cumin, pour over the potatoes, and toss. Season with salt and pepper.

3 Roast for 30–40 minutes, turning frequently with a metal spatula, until the potatoes are tender and have absorbed the liquid.

PREPARE AHEAD The potatoes can be prepared up to step 2 several hours before roasting.

6 servings

prep 10 mins
• cook 35–45 mins

ACCOMPANIMENTS

Roast sweet potato with sesame glaze

Roasting these vegetables brings out their natural sweetness.

INGREDIENTS

5 orange-fleshed sweet potatoes (yams), peeled
2 tbsp olive oil
salt and freshly ground black pepper
2 tbsp sesame seeds
1 tbsp honey
1 tbsp soy sauce

METHOD

1 Preheat the oven to 400°F (200°C). Cut the potatoes into large chunks and place on a baking sheet. Drizzle with the oil and season with salt and pepper. Roast the potatoes for 30 minutes, turning halfway through, until almost tender.

2 Mix together the sesame seeds, honey, and soy sauce. Pour over the sweet potatoes, and toss. Roast 20 minutes more, or until well glazed and tender.

6 servings

prep 10 mins
• cook 50 mins

Polenta

Smooth and creamy, soft polenta is the perfect foil for northern Italian dishes with meaty sauces.

INGREDIENTS

6 cups chicken or vegetable stock
$2^{1}/_{3}$ cups instant polenta
2 tbsp butter
$^{3}/_{4}$ cup freshly grated Parmesan, plus more to serve
salt and freshly ground black pepper

METHOD

1 In a large saucepan, heat the stock over high heat until almost boiling.

2 Gradually whisk in the polenta, then continue to whisk about 3 minutes, until the mixture is thick and soft. Add a little more stock or water, if necessary.

3 Stir in the butter and Parmesan, and season with salt and pepper. Serve immediately.

4 servings

prep 10 mins
• cook 10 mins

Grilled vegetables

Perfect for summer, these vegetables are easy to prepare and go well with any main dish.

INGREDIENTS

2 zucchini, halved lengthwise
1 large red bell pepper,
   quartered lengthwise and seeded
1 large yellow bell pepper,
   quartered lengthwise and seeded
1 large eggplant, sliced crosswise
1 fennel bulb, quartered lengthwise
$\frac{1}{2}$ cup olive oil, plus extra for brushing
3 tbsp balsamic vinegar
2 garlic cloves, chopped
$\frac{1}{4}$ cup coarsely chopped parsley,
   plus extra to garnish
salt and freshly ground black pepper

METHOD

1 Arrange the zucchini, red and yellow peppers, eggplant, and fennel, cut-sides up, in a large nonmetallic dish. Whisk together the oil, vinegar, garlic, parsley, and salt and pepper to taste. Spoon over the vegetables, and marinate at room temperature for at least 30 minutes.

2 Meanwhile, light an outdoor grill or preheat the broiler. Oil the grill grate or the broiler pan.

3 Lift the vegetables out of the marinade, and place them on the grill or broiler rack. Cook 3–5 minutes on each side, or until tender and lightly charred, brushing with the marinade. Serve warm or at room temperature, drizzled with remaining marinade and sprinkled with parsley.

PREPARE AHEAD The vegetables can marinate in step 1 for several hours. Or cook them a day in advance and serve at room temperature.

4 servings

**prep 20 mins,
plus marinating
• cook 4–6 mins**

**large, non-
metallic dish,
heat-resistant
pastry brush**

ACCOMPANIMENTS

Potato gratin

This baked potato dish is rich with cream and fragrant with garlic and nutmeg.

INGREDIENTS

2lb (900g) white- or red-skinned boiling potatoes
salt and freshly ground black pepper
2¹/₂ cups heavy cream
1 garlic clove, cut in half
pinch of freshly ground nutmeg
3 tbsp butter, at room temperature, cut up, plus more for the dish

METHOD

1 Preheat the oven to 350°F (180°C). Butter a 2qt (2 liter) shallow baking dish.

2 Peel the potatoes. Using a mandoline, a food processor fitted with a fine slicing blade, or a large knife, slice the potatoes into rounds about ¹/₈in (3mm) thick. Rinse the slices in cold water. Drain and pat dry with paper towels or a clean kitchen towel.

3 Place the potatoes in layers in the baking dish, seasoning with salt and pepper as you go.

4 Bring the cream, garlic, and nutmeg to a boil in a saucepan. Pour the cream over the potatoes. Dot the top with the butter.

5 Cover with aluminum foil. Bake about 1¹/₄ hours, or until the potatoes are just tender. Remove the foil. Increase the oven temperature to 450°F (250°C) and bake until the top is golden, about 10 minutes. Serve hot.

PREPARE AHEAD The potatoes can be peeled, sliced, and stored in water to cover for several hours.

4–6 servings

**prep 15–20 mins
• cook 1½ hrs**

**mandoline or
food processor
fitted with fine
slicing blade**

Ratatouille

This popular Mediterranean dish is delicious hot or cold.

INGREDIENTS

¼ cup olive oil
1 onion, chopped
1 zucchini, sliced
1 small eggplant, about 8oz (225g),
    cut into 1in (2.5cm) cubes
1 red bell pepper, seeded, cored,
    and cut into 1in (2.5cm) pieces
1 garlic clove, chopped
⅔ cup vegetable stock
one 14.5oz (411g) can chopped tomatoes
2 tsp chopped oregano, plus sprigs for garnish
salt and freshly ground black pepper

METHOD

1 Heat the oil in a large casserole over medium heat. Add the onion and cook for about 5 minutes, until soft and transparent. Stir in the zucchini, eggplant, red pepper, and garlic, and cook for 5 minutes, stirring occasionally, until the vegetables begin to soften.

2 Add the stock, tomatoes with their juices, and the chopped oregano and bring to a boil. Reduce the heat to low and partially cover the pan. Simmer about 25 minutes, stirring occasionally, until the vegetables are tender.

3 Add salt and black pepper to taste. Transfer to a serving bowl and serve immediately, garnished with oregano sprigs.

4 servings

prep 15 mins
• cook 40 mins

Tabbouleh

This Lebanese specialty of parsley, mint, tomatoes, and bulgur is refreshing all year round.

INGREDIENTS
³/₄ cup bulgur (cracked wheat)
boiling water, as needed
¹/₃ cup extra-virgin olive oil
¹/₄ cup fresh lemon juice
salt and freshly ground black pepper
4 scallions, finely chopped
¹/₂ cup chopped parsley
¹/₄ cup chopped mint
small lettuce leaves
2 ripe tomatoes, seeded, and finely diced

METHOD
1 Put the bulgur in a large bowl. Pour in enough boiling water to cover. Let stand about 10 minutes, or until the grains are swollen and tender. Drain in a fine wire sieve, rinse in cold water, and drain again.

2 Whisk the oil and lemon juice in a large bowl. Stir in bulgur. Season with salt and pepper.

3 Just before serving, mix in the scallions, parsley, and mint.

4 Arrange lettuce leaves on a serving dish. Spoon portions of tabbouleh into the leaves, scatter the diced tomatoes over the top and serve at room temperature.

4 servings

**prep 20 mins,
plus 15 mins
standing**

Spanish lentils

This Spanish lentil dish gets its deep flavor from chorizo, bacon, and paprika.

INGREDIENTS

1lb (450g) brown lentils, rinsed
  and drained
3oz (85g) smoked chorizo,
  thickly sliced
2 bay leaves
2 tbsp olive oil
2 garlic cloves, peeled

1 small slice rustic bread
salt
3oz (85g) slab bacon, thickly sliced
1 onion, finely chopped
1 tbsp all-purpose flour
1 tsp sweet paprika
1/2 cup vegetable stock or water

METHOD

1 Combine the lentils, chorizo, and bay leaves in a large saucepan with 1 quart (1 liter) water. Bring to a boil, then simmer for 35–40 minutes, or until the lentils are tender.

2 Meanwhile, heat 1 tbsp of the oil in a frying pan over medium-low heat. Add the garlic and cook for 2–3 minutes, stirring frequently, or until softened but not browned. Remove from the pan and reserve. Add the bread to the pan and fry over medium heat until lightly browned on both sides. Combine the bread and garlic in a food processor and process to produce coarse crumbs. Season with salt. Set the crumbs aside.

3 Add the remaining oil to the frying pan. Add the bacon and cook, stirring occasionally, about 5 minutes, until browned. Add the onion and cook for 3 minutes more, until the onion is tender. Sprinkle with the flour and paprika and stir well. Stir in the stock and bring to a boil. Reduce the heat to low and simmer for 2 minutes. Keep warm.

4 Drain the lentils and return to the saucepan. Stir in the garlic crumbs and the bacon mixture. Reheat, adding water if needed to moisten the lentils. Transfer to a serving dish and serve hot.

PREPARE AHEAD The dish can be refrigerated for up to 1 day and reheated.

6 servings

**prep 15 mins
• cook 1 hr**

Egg fried rice

This popular Chinese-style rice dish is an excellent way to use up leftover rice.

INGREDIENTS
1 tbsp vegetable oil
2 scallions, sliced
1 green or red bell pepper,
    cored, seeded, and diced
4–6 cups cold cooked rice
2 eggs, beaten
2 tbsp soy sauce

METHOD
1 Heat the wok or large frying pan over a high heat until very hot. Add the oil and swirl around. Add the scallions and pepper and stir–fry for 2 minutes, or until softened but not colored.

2 Add the rice to the wok and stir-fry about 5 minutes until heated through. Push the rice away from the center of the wok, pour in the eggs, and stir until scrambled and set.

3 Once the eggs are scrambled, toss all the ingredients together, add the soy sauce, and serve.

4–6 servings

**prep 5 mins
• cook 10 mins**

**make sure
the rice is
cold, not
freshly made**

wok

Glazed carrots with thyme

These carrots are a good accompaniment to roast beef, pork, lamb, or poultry.

INGREDIENTS
1lb (450g) carrots, thinly sliced
grated zest of 1 orange
¼ cup fresh orange juice
1½ tbsp butter
1 tbsp brown sugar
1 garlic clove, crushed and peeled
salt and freshly ground black pepper
½ tsp chopped thyme

METHOD

1 Place the carrots, orange zest and juice, butter, sugar, and garlic in a small saucepan, and season with salt and pepper. Add enough cold water to barely cover the carrots.

2 Bring to a boil, then cover and cook over a medium-high heat for 8–10 minutes, or until the carrots are just tender.

3 Remove the cover and boil until all the liquid has evaporated and the carrots are glazed and golden at the edges, shaking the pan occasionally to prevent sticking. Just before serving, sprinkle in the thyme leaves.

PREPARE AHEAD Complete through the end of step 2 several hours in advance, then finish cooking just before serving.

4 servings

prep 10 mins
• cook 15 mins

Braised red cabbage with apple

Most cabbage varieties are best cooked quickly, but red cabbage is an exception, benefiting from long, slow cooking.

INGREDIENTS

2 bacon slices, diced
1 onion, finely chopped
1 tbsp sugar
1 tart apple, such as Granny Smith,
    peeled, cored, and chopped
2lb (900g) shredded red cabbage
$\frac{1}{4}$ cup red wine vinegar
salt and freshly ground black pepper

METHOD

1 In a large frying pan over medium-low heat, cook the bacon until it renders its fat. Add the onion, and cook for about 5 minutes, or until softened. Add the sugar and cook for 5 minutes, until the onion is golden. Add the apple and cover. Cook, stirring occasionally, for about 3–4 minutes, until the apple is crisp-tender.

2 Add the cabbage and toss to coat thoroughly with the bacon fat. Add the vinegar, and mix well. Cover and cook over low heat for 10 minutes, or until the cabbage becomes a shade lighter.

3 Stir in $\frac{2}{3}$ cup water and season with salt and pepper. Cover and simmer over medium-low heat for 1–1$\frac{1}{4}$ hours, stirring occasionally, until the cabbage is very tender. Add a little more water, if necessary. Just before serving, season again with salt and pepper. Serve hot.

4 servings

prep 10 mins
• cook 1hr 25
mins–1 hr 30
mins

Ultimate mashed potatoes

Potatoes with a twist. This richly flavored side makes a valuable contribution to the perfect roast dinner.

INGREDIENTS

3lb (1.35kg) baking potatoes,
    such as Burbank, peeled and cubed
salt and freshly ground black pepper
2 tbsp heavy cream
2 tbsp whole milk
6 tbsp butter
1 cup (4oz/115g) shredded Cheddar
4 scallions, white and green parts, chopped
2 tbsp chopped parsley
2 tbsp finely chopped chives
1 tbsp prepared horseradish

METHOD

1 Place the potatoes in a large saucepan and add cold water to cover. Bring to a boil and add a little salt. Cover and reduce the heat to medium. Cook at a brisk simmer for 20–30 minutes, or until tender.

2 Drain well. Return to low heat and stir for a minute or two to evaporate excess liquid.

3 Add the cream, milk, and butter and mash. Add the Cheddar, scallions, parsley, chives, and horseradish and mix well. Season with salt and pepper and serve hot.

6 servings

**prep 10 mins
• cook 45 mins**

ACKNOWLEDGMENTS

DK PUBLISHING WOULD LIKE TO THANK THE FOLLOWING:

Photographers
Carole Tuff, Tony Cambio, William Shaw, Stuart West, David Munns, David Murray, Adrian Heapy, Nigel Gibson, Kieran Watson, Roddy Paine, Gavin Sawyer, Ian O'Leary, Steve Baxter, Martin Brigdale, Francesco Guillamet, Jeff Kauck, William Reavell

Picture Research
Emma Shepherd

Index
Susan Bosanko

Useful information

Roasting poultry

Use these times as a guide, bearing in mind the size and weight of each bird vary. Be sure to preheat the oven before cooking your bird(s), and always check that the bird is fully cooked before serving.

MEAT		OVEN TEMPERATURE	COOKING TIME
Poussin		375°F (190°C)	12 mins per 1lb (450g) plus 12 mins
Chicken		400°F (200°C)	20 mins per 1lb (450g) plus 20 mins
Duck		350°F (180°C)	20 mins per 1lb (450g) plus 20 mins
Goose		350°F (180°C)	20 mins per 1lb (450g) plus 20 mins
Pheasant		400°F (200°C)	50 mins total cooking
Turkey	7–9lb (3.5–4.5kg)	375°F (190°C)	2½–3 hrs total cooking
	10–12lb (5–6kg)	375°F (190°C)	3½–4 hrs total cooking
	13–17lb (6.5–8.5kg)	375°F (190°C)	4½–5 hrs total cooking

Oven temperature equivalents

FAHRENHEIT	CELSIUS	DESCRIPTION
225°F	110°C	Cool
250°F	130°C	Cool
275°F	140°C	Very low
300°F	150°C	Very low
325°F	160°C	Low
350°F	180°C	Moderate
375°F	190°C	Moderately hot
400°F	200°C	Hot
425°F	220°C	Hot
450°F	230°C	Very hot
475°F	240°C	Very hot